JEREMY

BY
MAGARET JEAN RALSTON

ACKNOWLEDGMENT

I want to express my deepest gratitude to my family and friends who stood by me during the emotional journey of writing this book. To my children, grandchildren, and great-grandson, your love and support have been my anchor. A special thanks to those who knew Jeremy, whose memories and stories enriched these pages. This book is a tribute not only to my brother but to anyone who has faced the silent struggles of life. Thank you for helping me honor Jeremy's memory.

DEDICATION

To Jeremy, my beloved brother, whose life was a testament to resilience and creativity. Though your struggles were immense, your spirit continues to shine through these pages. You are forever missed and cherished.

ABOUT THE AUTHOR

Margret J. Ralston is a devoted mother of four, grandmother to eight, and a proud great-grandmother. With a career in healthcare, she has dedicated her life to helping others while nurturing her family. Writing has always been a passion, but this book holds a special place in her heart. Written as a memorial to her brother Jeremy, it is a heartfelt tribute to his life, struggles, and the legacy he left behind.

"You carried burdens that were invisible to us all. I wish I could have been your light in those dark moments. I will honor your memory by sharing your story."

If tears could build a stairway
And memories were a lane.
We would walk right up to Heaven.
And bring you back again.

No farewell words were spoken,
No time to say goodbye;
You were gone before we knew it —
And only you know why.

Our hearts still ache in sadness,
And secret tears still flow.
What it meant to lose you
No one will ever know.

But now we know you want us.
To mourn for you no more;
To remember all our happy times
Life still has more in store.

Since you'll never be forgotten
We hold for you today.

A hallowed happy place

Within our hearts

Is where you'll always stay.

— Jennifer Johann

Poem:
In the Quiet

In the quiet of the night, I write,

Words like whispers, soft as light.

Memories dance, a gentle sigh,

On every page, I see you fly.

Brother, you're a star, so bright,

Guiding me through the darkest night.

Though time has passed, the years have passed,

In every heartbeat, your love will last.

Table of Contents

INTRODUCTION

Our family started back in the early 1940s. Jeremy Elliott Applegate was born Paul Andrew Boyce in San Jose California. Jeremy was the youngest child in the family and my brother David was the oldest. David was born in 1943 and Jeremy in 1965, so we covered a wide range of ages. There were eleven kids in our family. Jeremy left home at a young age and lived with other family members off and on until finally, he went missing for sixteen years. We never saw him again. We all thought he was working and making it big in Hollywood. I did not hear about his death until the time my mother was dying, when a family member looked Jeremy up on a website and we learned of his suicide. I was totally devastated; it was like a bad dream and I just wanted to wake up and find out it wasn't true.

Jeremy always wanted to be an actor. He appeared in numerous television shows and movies but just in small parts. His biggest break was in the movie "Heathers," in which he played the part of an editor working on the school paper.

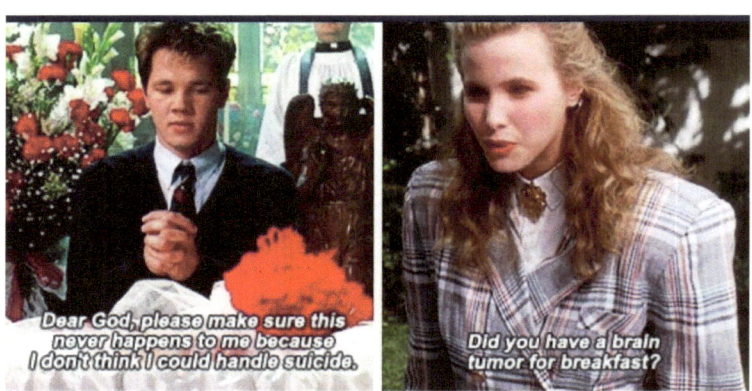

Dear God, please make sure this never happens to me because I don't think I could handle suicide.

Did you have a brain tumor for breakfast?

Two stars of the movie *Heathers* died at an early age: Jeremy Applegate (Peter Dawson, whose character prays he will never commit suicide) committed suicide with a shotgun on March 23, 2000, and Kim Walker (Heather Chandler, who had the line "Did you have a brain tumor for breakfast?") died of a brain tumor on March 6, 2001.

#damn #heathers knew what was up

He never really made it big. Most days he was depressed, and he frequently failed to show up for auditions. As part of his therapy, the doctors told him to avoid contact with his family. The medications he was taking made him paranoid. Jeremy was in and out of mental hospitals for years. We are still trying to find out the details of his medical troubles.

I decided to write this book as a memorial to my beloved brother. To show Jeremy how much I loved him, how much I miss him - and how much I wish I could have been a bigger part of his life.

- Peggy Ralston

CHAPTER ONE.
CHILDHOOD

Jeremy Applegate's birth name was Paul Andrew Boyce. He was born August 29, 1965, in San Jose, California, and was named after Paul McCartney. He was the last-born child in a family with five brothers and four sisters. Paul was born with the bilabial cord wrapped around his neck and he could easily have died. He had blond hair and blue eyes. He was a beautiful baby, but our mother did not want another child. Mother didn't care for or want children. Back in those days, birth control was unheard of. Mother bore a child every two years, so she must have been pregnant thirteen times.

When Paul was brought home from the hospital, it was up to his brothers and sisters to care for him. As a baby, Mother would leave him alone for hours crying. I couldn't stand it ... so every night one of us would sneak in his room and bring him to sleep with us. Mother would scream, "Get the baby down here now!" No one wanted to answer her, we were afraid.

Then the next day, we would have to go to school hated to leave Paul with our mother. She frequently left little Paul alone many times during the day. Once, my oldest brother David had a job interview, so he took Paul with him. We all took turns taking care of the baby wherever we could- except when we were in school and couldn't take Paul with us.

When I would come home from school, Paul would still be in his crib screaming and sobbing, sopping wet and lying in a soaked sheet. I don't remember that our mother ever changed his diapers. God but we just hated the way she treated Paul! That poor baby would bang his head on the crib so hard that the bars were coming loose. Mother would yell, "Paul stop that!" We would find bruises and red marks on his body as well as very bad diaper rash. This went on for years until he was able to walk.

Jeremy

Jeremy: Memories of an Actor

One day when I came home from school calling for Paul, he was nowhere in sight. I was terribly worried because I couldn't find him anywhere. So, I went looking from room to room — until I finally found him sleeping under my sister's bed. He was terrified of Mother and had been hiding there under the bed until he fell asleep. One day, I saw Mother slap Paul terribly hard, but he did not cry. So, she just kept slapping him on the face. She said, "Why don't you cry, Paul? — you must like being slapped ..."

But he would not cry. His face was so red that she left her hand marks on his face from slapping so hard. She raised her hand to slap him again, but my sister Rosemary blocked her hand and said, "Stop it — he's just a baby!" Mother turned to my sister with that devil look in her eyes, raised her foot, and kicked Rosemary in the crotch, bringing her to her knees. It was so painful that I had to help Rosemary stand up.

Jeremy

Mother even made Paul save his urine in large glass containers in his closet. We never knew what that was all about.

My brothers and I had to do all the grocery shopping. We took Paul with us to protect him and try to keep him safe.

Mother would talk to herself and then answer back too — just as if there was someone else in the room. She never wanted Paul. Mother told everyone that he was an accident, a change of a life child. Paul needed a real Mother; he needed love. He needed clothing and food that was not rotten and discarded. Paul never had what a normal family should have provided. None of us ever had those things. My brothers and sisters tried their best, but we were just kids ourselves. It was as if we were trying to be adults but were trapped in children's bodies — and fighting so hard to get out. All of us kids took turns dressing Paul and buying clothes for him.

Jeremy

In the summertime, we would take Paul to the beach. He would go everywhere with us as if he was our own child.

Jeremy

When my brother and I took him visiting friends, they thought he was my son.

***

My father is a kind and gentle man; he never knew that Paul was being abused. He did what he could to provide for his family. Dad worked two jobs six days a week. He earned a fair amount, but Mother hid the money she should have been spending on us. Dad once bought Paul a great toy — a battery-operated car, which in the 1960s was the latest thing. Paul had fun riding that around the house.

When Paul was two, his brother David took him to the zoo and cared for him as he was his own child. David took him to the Santa Cruz boardwalk to play on the rides. It was the closest Pacific Ocean Park. He had fun listening to the bands play their music on the beach. David took him to see the dinosaur rise in and out of the water, it turned to the right while growling, and then it went back down under the water. Paul watched for hours with his brother David. He loved the beach and went there often.

Whenever Paul had company, Mother would put on her phony face and act as if she was a great mom. As soon as his friends left, she would begin slapping him around and calling him terrible names you should never say to an adult, much less a child. He was only three years old.

***

In 1968 when I was eighteen, Paul was to be the ring-bearer at my wedding, but he was so terrified he couldn't do it. After I moved out of the house, Mother would frequently drop Paul off to stay with me. I didn't know why; I guess she didn't want to deal with him. So, I potty-trained him and tried to help him as much as I could. When it came time for Mother to pick him up again, he would scream and say, "Please, I want to stay! Don't make me go with her..."

Jeremy

It tore me up inside to see him go. If I'd had my way, I would never have let him go. If only things had been different maybe he might have been able to lead a normal life. What is a normal life? We all never had that. Paul was a child born to a sick sociopath we all had to call Mother.

When Paul was four, he had hours of fun with his brother Richard, who took him to picnics and amusement park rides. Paul had fun going on to high school outings with his brother. Richard showed off Paul to his high school sweetheart. When they went on hay rides, friends would ask Richard if Paul was his own son. Maybe it was because they looked so much alike and got along so well together.

***

As he grew older, Paul began abusing the family pets which is a typical response from a child who has been abused himself. There were cats everywhere in the house. Once Paul grabbed a few kittens put them in kitchen canisters filled with sugar water and left them in there until they were dead. When Paul was about five years old, his older brother Brian took him to the railroad track, where he took his Diaper Dan doll to the tracks.

Another time, Paul was playing with his older brother Brian. Paul was chasing Brian, and as they passed through the kitchen, Paul picked up a butcher knife. He ran after Brian with the knife, waving it in the air and cutting Brian's shirt-but the knife never broke the skin.

Once when Paul was about eight years old, I found him in the living room with a rope around his neck and choking. I was so shocked I screamed, "What have you done? Oh my god!" as I untangled the rope from his throat.

Was this an accident? - Or did he want to die even then?

Jeremy

If I had not been at home, he would have died.

***

Rosemary often took Paul shopping and dressed him in the best clothes. They spent time at the park playing ball, throwing a Frisbee around, or flying kites. Rosemary is the sister who named Paul after one of the Beatles.

Paul made his own homemade Claymation movie at the age of ten using an old movie projector. Joey was the star of the movie. Paul would move Joey every few inches take a picture, and move his arms and legs as if he were a real person. He did this throughout the whole movie. In the end, Joey was destroyed blown up into a million pieces.

I had that movie he made, but Mother threw it out.

Paul was so creative. He was always role-playing, and we all thought he was meant to be an actor.

Jeremy

Sister Marian played board games with Paul and took him on airplane rides. Marian baked him his favorite cookies which were chocolate chip and peanut butter. Paul spent every other weekend with Marian having the best time ever.

When Paul was twelve, his brother Philip played football with him, took him to the beach, taught and him to ride his first bike. They had so much fun together that they did not want the days to end. Sometimes Paul would spend the night at Philip's house.

Brother Brian was eight years older than Paul. They spent a lot of time together doing guy things. Some of it is good some not.

Paul tagged along with Brian wherever he went.

CHAPTER TWO
JOEY

Paul had a made-up imaginary friend he called Joey. He would talk to him for hours. I guess that was the only outlet he had to escape his own abusive life. Whenever Paul would play house, he would set another place for Joey. He made up a dummy and dressed him in his own clothes. It was as if he was acting out his own movie.

Brother Dennis loved Paul like his own son. They went on a lot of fishing trips to the Santa Cruz River. Dennis took him on his first visit to the San Francisco Zoo. In that year, the zoo started charging for admission which was one dollar. Dennis spent hours with Paul looking at all the exotic animals. They had a lot of fun that day. Paul loved it and wanted to visit again.

Paul was very intelligent for his age. The teachers at his school couldn't believe how bright he was at seven years old. He once made an anatomically correct model of his body out of playdough, molding the outside first and then opening it up to make all the internal organs too.

He would stay over every weekend at the house of one of his brothers or sisters. He loved to visit us because he would be very well cared for. He had someone else to play with besides just himself. When Mother came to pick him up, he would hide because he didn't want to go. He would cry and go into a rage. He would grab a hold of my leg and would not let go. He was getting into the car screaming, "Please help me I do not want to go home" There was nothing I could do.

CHAPTER THREE.
ALWAYS HUNGRY

Paul didn't have much to eat as a child. His bedroom was like a pigsty, and there was mold in the refrigerator covering the food like a blanket. The stench was terrible; Mother never cleaned it, it made your stomach upset. Poor Paul would say, "Please can you get some food in this house?"— And she would reply, "The food is still good, just wash it off." She didn't care if he got sick. Paul would use her charge card to order pizza. Mother would not find out until later when she got the bill in the mail. He would steal money out of her purse for food.

***

One day the school nurse phoned because Paul had passed out. Mother showed up at the nurse's office just as the nurse was giving him smelling salts. "Oh, Paul!" she said. "What happened, Sweetie?"

Paul just gave her a dirty look.

As they were walking to the car, Mother said, "You fool! What the Hell is wrong with you? I don't want anyone to know what goes on in our household."

Paul was very depressed; he had hoped that someone would find out about his home life so that he would not have to live with her anymore. Mother went wild with rage because she'd had to pick him up from school. She told him to clean up the house.

He was still terribly hungry, for he had not eaten since the previous night. How could he get something to eat without her seeing him?

Paul called me at home, and I picked him up at the corner. He was crying. "I hate Mother! I'm so hungry, I'm feeling sick..." So, I fixed him a sandwich and a bowl of chicken noodle soup, which he wolfed down because he was starving. Poor Paul- I wanted so badly to keep him with me.

Jeremy

I took care of Paul like he was my own child. Paul was only four years older than my son John, and they grew up together. They spent hours together riding bikes, swimming, and role-playing. We spent a lot of time making Christmas ornaments out of play dough. After the ornaments were baked Paul and my son would paint them. Then get them ready to hang on the tree.

Paul made Christmas ornaments from playdough. He was very much into detail, and once made a model of Santa Claus. Paul insisted that it had the right colors, the meticulous—correct size, and precise shape.

By this time, Paul was the only one left home with Mother. My brothers and sisters all felt very sorry for him and would bake Paul cookies and real home-cooked meals.

CHAPTER FOUR.
ILLNESS

Paul had very bad allergies complicated with asthma due to the stress he was under, and to the filth of the house he was living in. He frequently had to be taken to the hospital emergency room because of his asthma attacks. Paul was there so often that Dad rented a nebulizer machine for him so he could breathe.

My brother's dream was to have a mother who loved him and would take care of him; the dream of having a normal family life. However, we all knew that was just a dream and would never happen. Paul's heath always improved whenever he was not at— home when he was happy.

Many of us in the family had illnesses as children from lack of food and improper care. Some of my siblings had arthritis so crippling that they used crutches. Others had nosebleeds from poor eating and lack of proper food.

Sometimes all Paul could find in the house was milk, and he would drink that until he was full. Back in the 1960s, milk was delivered to your door in glass bottles — so Paul would order extra things from the milkman, such as orange juice, chocolate milk, cottage cheese, and popsicles. That was one way of getting enough to eat. Paul was very clever about getting food — until he was caught by Mother. Then he would start using her credit card to make phone orders so he could eat. He ordered more pizzas, fast foods, or anything he could in order to eat.

***

One time when Paul was having a severe asthma attack, Mother said, "Get out of here. I never wanted you anyway..." So, he called my sister Rosemary, who took him to the hospital. It was an especially bad attack this time, and Paul had to spend the night in the hospital. The next day when he came home, Mother screamed, "You're no good for nothing you're a pain in my ass!"

Mother would run around the house chasing Jeremy with the broom and hitting him as hard as she could. She would chase him down to the basement and then lock the door behind him. Jeremy got out through a small window it was a tight fit, but he got it out safely. Jeremy called a friend to pick him up.

Susan's abuse went on until my parents divorced in 1980 when my mother kicked Paul out of the house for good. He was only fourteen years old.

CHAPTER FIVE.
MOVING OUT

When Mother threw Paul out of the house, Dad called our older sister Susan. Dad wanted to get Paul away from Mother before something terrible happened. So, Paul went to live with Susan in Hayward, California when he was fourteen years old. He enrolled at a local school and got a job as a newspaper boy so he could earn some money of his own. It was not much but — at least it was something.

Susan helped Paul get his first paper route. She also helped him get his driver's license when he was sixteen years old. She took him fishing and they did a lot of outdoor activities. Susan and Paul baked cookies and prepared meals together and had tremendous fun doing it.

Paul took Driver's Education; he loved cars and knew all their ins and outs. He stayed with Susan until he was sixteen years old, and then moved on. For a while, he lived with his brother Dennis in Santa Clara. But Paul was too much for Dennis to handle, so again he had to move on. Paul next lived with brother Philip, but Philip had more responsibilities than he could handle. So finally, Paul called me. This was quite a surprise, as I was living in Oregon at the time.

He said, "Peggy, I want to move in with you." I thought he was joking; but the next day, I heard a knock at my front door. It was Paul. I was very surprised and said, "You weren't kidding about moving in!"

Paul had just earned his driver's license and made the eight-hour drive from San Jose, California to Bend, Oregon overnight. He drove a white 1960 LeSabre station wagon, which was in pretty good shape for such an old car. Paul took very good care of that car; he changed the oil, tuned up the engine, and bled the brakes. He also tuned up my car.

Jeremy

***

We had a lot of great times together. We waited in line for hours to see movies like *E.T.* and *Blue Lagoon*. Paul loved living with my family. He started taking acting classes at the town theater in Bend, Oregon that year.

Then I had a call from my sister Susan, who also needed a place to live. So, she moved in too. At first, it was really nice having both my brother and sister living with my family. But then one day Paul and Susan got into a big fight, with a lot of fist-hitting, slapping, and screaming. I think Paul was jealous of Susan living with me.

Paul punched Susan in the eye! He was in trouble now. Susan's eye was badly swollen and didn't look good. The next day, Paul began acting mean to everyone. Susan left and moved in with a friend. We did not hear from her for a long time after that.

Jeremy

Then one day, Paul was playing with one of my daughters. Jeanette was eleven years old at the time. Paul was pretending to slap Jeanette across the face. She was wearing braces. When I saw Jeanette's face bleeding, I was furious. "What the hell is the matter with you? Why did you do that?" I was so mad that I told him he had to leave.

I did not mean it literally, but Paul took it that way.

My brother moved out. He was gone. I was very upset not knowing where he was. Later in the day, I received a phone call from Paul. "I'm living at a friend's house now," he said. "Don't worry about me — I'm okay."

I wondered whether he was really okay — or was he just saying that so I wouldn't worry?

CHAPTER SIX.
PAUL BECOMES JEREMY

The next day I met Paul at his friend's house. We had lunch together at a shopping mall and saw a movie. Then it was getting late and I had to pick up my kids from school. I saw Paul a few more times that year. Finally, I heard from one of my sisters that he had moved away.

Rosemary said that when she mailed Paul a Christmas card that year, she put her address and phone number inside. He called and thanked her for the card. That was the last time she heard from him. Paul called other relatives and asked if he could stay with them because he had no place to go. Nobody said yes. None of us ever heard from Paul after that...

***

I learned later that my brother changed his name from Paul Andrew Boyce to Jeremy Elliott Applegate at the Deschutes County Courthouse in Oregon on

Jeremy

September 1, 1983. He took his middle name from the character Elliott in the movie *E.T.*

Paul called Dad and asked if he should try acting. Dad said, "Sure, give it a try." That was the last time Dad talked to my brother. No one in our family heard from Paul ever again. It seemed he had disappeared off the face of the Earth — didn't stay in contact with any of his family or friends.

Then in 1988, I was watching a Movie of the Week one night on television. It was called *Scandal*, starred Rachel Welsh, and was set in a small town. I like Rachel Welsh so I watched it.

Half an hour into the movie, I saw my brother Paul playing a high-school student talking to Rachel Welsh's daughter.

I could not believe my eyes. I turned on the VCR and I taped the show. I was so excited and happy for him that he was making it as an actor.

CHAPTER SEVEN
AN ACTOR AT LAST

Over the years, Jeremy Applegate had parts in a few motion pictures. Throughout the 1980s, he had numerous guest stars and recurring roles on television shows like *My Two Dads*, *Our House*, and *21 Jump Street*. He appeared in *Heathers* (1989) as Peter Dawson. In 1994, he was in the television movie *Lies of the Heart: The Story of Laurie Kellogg*. Jeremy was also in *Strange Teen* (1996) and *The Cable Guy* (1996). He also appeared in a few commercials for Long John Silvers. After that, we didn't see him on television or in any movies.

***

Over the years that have passed since then, we have heard from a number of my brother's friends. The following information is based on what they told us:

Jeremy

Kim Giles wrote to me about the years my brother was missing, and I got information from letters Jeremy wrote to her. She helped fill in some of the blanks.

Jeremy Applegate made up a fictitious background for his early life. He told people that he was born May 10, 1968, in Texas... That his real parents were very rich and were killed in an airplane crash when he was very young... After his parents' death, he was left in an orphanage... He ran away to Hollywood to become an actor.

Kim told me that Jeremy liked to work on cars. He had a BMW and he could fix and knew every part of his car. He was a whiz on the computer. He had a nose job in 1997 because he had a lot of trouble breathing and his nose was too wide on the sides.

He lived in twenty-four different places since first arriving in Los Angeles in 1984. He didn't have the energy or the inclination to find anywhere else to live.

Jeremy had a degenerative disk disorder in his neck that was the result of a motorcycle accident. Jeremy tried acupuncture. The doctor put eleven needles in the lump in his neck – and it really worked so that he could go on casting interviews.

When facing adversity, Jeremy would fight to the end – but whenever he lost, he would say, "I'm going to kill myself." He was frequently suicidal and seeing a psychiatrist. He was taking Xanax as well as many other prescription drugs. He was in and out of mental hospitals all of his adult life.

***

Jeremy had two cats – named Clarice and Febe. He loved his cats, and they provided the only affection he ever got. Jeremy named his cat Clarice after Clarice Starling in *Silence of the Lambs*. The other cat, Febe, was one of Clarice's babies.

The only things Jeremy really liked were watching *South Park* and *Star Trek* on television. He was definitely a Trekkie – and even had his own Starfleet uniform. He liked Buddy Holly, Chinese food, Italian food, and coffee. He did not drink alcohol but smoked marijuana every day around 4:00 PM. Jeremy had a 2002 BMW which he converted into a 1969 model. He liked working on it and making it go fast.

He was always very unhappy and frequently suicidal. I read in some of his letters that he would put his gun in his mouth, unlock the trigger – then do some hard thinking then take it out. He hated himself. He smoked a lot of pot.

My brother wrote a letter to his landlord about this neighbor, after which Singh changed completely and began asking Jeremy to drive him around to get parts for his car. It was bizarre.

Jeremy

***

Jeremy called his doctor's office for a refill on his medication, stating that he was suicidal and wanted to talk with the doctor. The nurse refused; he called her a bitch and she hung up. The nurse told the answering service not to take any messages from Jeremy. He finally got hold of the doctor and explained to him what was going on. About a week later, Jeremy received a certified letter from his doctor stating that he would no longer treat Jeremy. No explanation was given, and Jeremy's phone calls were never returned.

***

Jeremy had problems with his landlord, Mr. Chin. The man put notes on Jeremy's car saying that the car was abandoned, which was not the case. He put a warning card on Jeremy's BMW to move it every 72 hours or the car would be picked up. When a meter maid came and impounded the car, Jeremy had to pay a $160.00 fine.

Mr. Chin hadn't changed the locks on the apartment when Jeremy moved in. Jeremy didn't complain — he was just relieved to have a roof over his head. So, he took it upon himself to purchase new locks and install them. About a week after that, he lost his keys. He thought they were probably lost in the mess of his room. Therefore, he re-keyed the locks to save Chin money and took it off his rent. When he called the property owner and told him about the new locks, Chin became very upset.

So Jeremy paid the rent for that month — but the very next day, Chin slipped the check back under the door. Jeremy called to find out what the problem was and left numerous messages.

Jeremy received no return calls. On May 11, 1998, the landlord gave him a 3-day notice to pay or quit. This was also slipped under the door. It didn't make sense because Jeremy had paid and the landlord returned the money. Then on May 26, Jeremy was served with eviction papers that said he had five days to respond or the sheriff would remove him forcibly.

All this affected Jeremy very badly, making him more suicidal, depressed, and unable to sleep. He was vomiting, running a 102-degree temperature, and had high blood pressure. Jeremy tried to get his allergy shots but his blood pressure was too high. The allergy nurse was worried about him; it was nice that Jeremy had someone who cared about what happened to him.

Jeremy had a lot of worries. He tried to get legal advice, but the low-income programs were shut down. His medical problems were erratic. He would feel okay one day — then his mood would change and he'd hate himself as well as anyone who'd ever hurt him. He slept all day, missed two calls from his agent, and then went back to sleep depressed again.

Jeremy

He hated his life, having to hang on all day and then doing it all over again the next day.

Life was really bad for Jeremy. He called his friends and told them he was going to end it all. They thought he was just crying wolf — but in reality, he was crying for help. If only someone had checked his background and found out where he really came from... maybe we could have found him and helped.

Jeremy just wanted a place to call his own and to have good friends he could count on. However, that never happened to him. Jeremy had to fight for life from the very beginning to the bitter end — and the struggle eventually killed him.

He stood up for what he thought was right. He was very intelligent. What Jeremy wanted, was a normal life — but in his own view, he was an only child orphaned at a very young age.

Jeremy

Jeremy had many problems with people in positions of authority. He could not and would not take orders from anyone, largely because he was bipolar — manic depressive — as well as schizophrenic. When Jeremy was suicidal, he would take the trigger-lock off his shotgun and put the barrel into his mouth.

He was terrified with nightmares. This may have been a side effect of the Mirtazapine medication he was on. He wished that the Grays from UFOs would take him away so he wouldn't have to follow rules ever again. He talked about space aliens and believed they were real.

Jeremy never told any of his friends the true story of his life and family. If only he had contacted one of us — we would have tried to help. He needed his family, but his doctors thought that would be a big mistake. The doctors over-medicated him. The last mental hospital where Jeremy was last treated was in Pasadena — a hospital well-known to the Hollywood stars — but which has had hundreds of complaints on how they handle patients there.

Jeremy just wanted the pain to go away. It was Christmas, and he hated spending holidays alone. He thought it out carefully this time. He was going to end the pain, he could not go on anymore.

He made one final call to a friend to say that he was going to end it all. His friend called the police and told them what was going on. The police phoned Jeremy — but he didn't care anymore. He had made up his mind that life was not worth living. Jeremy Applegate put the shotgun in his mouth, and pulled back the trigger-lock as he had done so many times before.

CHAPTER EIGHT.
PROBLEMS

Jeremy had arguments with his next-door neighbor, a man named Singh, who claimed that Jeremy had parked in his parking space. Singh left two nasty notes threatening Jeremy if he parked there again. When Jeremy tried to reason with Singh, the man started screaming in his face, becoming increasingly violent. So, Jeremy took out a canister of tear gas as a precaution. Singh saw this and tried to force his way into Jeremy's apartment. Jeremy chased him off with the tear gas.

The next day when Jeremy went out to the mailbox, this neighbor started to provoke him again. Jeremy took out his tear gas, so Singh ran inside and dialed 911. Then Singh told my brother, "Don't go anywhere — they are coming for you!" Two police squad cars showed up and Singh told them that Jeremy had threatened him for no reason. He went on ranting about the parking space. The police realized that Singh was a psycho and told Jeremy, "If he gets out of control again, give him a good dose of that tear gas."

Jeremy had many problems with people in positions of authority. He could not and would not take orders from anyone, largely because he was bipolar — manic depressive — as well as schizophrenic. When Jeremy was suicidal, he would take the trigger-lock off his shotgun and put the barrel into his mouth.

He was terrified with nightmares. This may have been a side effect of the Mirtazapine medication he was on. He wished that the Grays from UFOs would take him away so he wouldn't have to follow rules ever again. He talked about space aliens and believed they were real.

Jeremy never told any of his friends the true story of his life and family. If only he had contacted one of us — we would have tried to help. He needed his family, but his doctors thought that would be a big mistake. The doctors over-medicated him. The last mental hospital where Jeremy was last treated was in Pasadena — a hospital well-known to the Hollywood stars — but which has had hundreds of complaints on how they handle patients there.

Jeremy just wanted the pain to go away. It was Christmas, and he hated spending holidays alone. He thought it out carefully this time. He was going to end the pain; he could not go on anymore.

He made one final call to a friend to say that he was going to end it all. His friend called the police and told them what was going on. The police phoned Jeremy — but he didn't care anymore. He had made up his mind that life was not worth living. Jeremy Applegate put the shotgun in his mouth and pulled back the trigger-lock as he had done so many times before.

Jeremy

My brother wrote a letter to his landlord about this neighbor, after which Singh changed completely and began asking Jeremy to drive him around to get parts for his car. It was bizarre.

***

Jeremy called his doctor's office for a refill on his medication, stating that he was suicidal and wanted to talk with the doctor. The nurse refused; he called her a bitch and she hung up. The nurse told the answering service not to take any messages from Jeremy. He finally got hold of the doctor and explained to him what was going on. About a week later, Jeremy received a certified letter from his doctor stating that he would no longer treat Jeremy. No explanation was given, and Jeremy's phone calls were never returned.

***

Jeremy

Jeremy had problems with his landlord, Mr. Chin. The man put notes on Jeremy's car saying that the car was abandoned. This was not the case... He put a warning card on Jeremy's BMW to move it every 72 hours or the car would be picked up. When a meter maid came and impounded the car, Jeremy had to pay a $160.00 fine.

Mr. Chin hadn't changed the locks on the apartment when Jeremy moved in. Jeremy didn't complain — he was just relieved to have a roof over his head. So, he took it upon himself to purchase new locks and install them. About a week after that, he lost his keys. He thought they were probably lost in the mess of his room. Therefore, he re-keyed the locks to save Chin money and took it off his rent. When he called the property owner and told him about the new locks, Chin became very upset.

So, Jeremy paid the rent for that month — but the very next day, Chin slipped the check back under the door. Jeremy called to find out what the problem was and left numerous messages — Jeremy had many problems with people in positions of authority. He could not and would not take orders from anyone, largely because he was bipolar — manic depressive — as well as schizophrenic. When Jeremy was suicidal, he would take the trigger-lock off his shotgun and put the barrel into his mouth.

He was terrified with nightmares. This may have been a side effect of the Mirtazapine medication he was on. He wished that the Grays from UFOs would take him away so he wouldn't have to follow rules ever again. He talked about space aliens and believed they were real.

Jeremy never told any of his friends the true story of his life and family. If only he had contacted one of us — we would have tried to help. He needed his family, but his doctors thought that would be a big mistake. The doctors over-medicated him. The last mental hospital where Jeremy was last treated was in Pasadena — a hospital well-known to the Hollywood stars — but which has had hundreds of complaints on how they handle patients there.

Jeremy just wanted the pain to go away. It was Christmas, and he hated spending holidays alone. He thought it out carefully this time. He was going to end the pain; he could not go on anymore.

He made one final call to a friend to say that he was going to end it all. His friend called the police and told them what was going on. The police phoned Jeremy — but he didn't care anymore. He had made up his mind that life was not worth living. Jeremy Applegate put the shotgun in his mouth, and pulled back the trigger-lock as he had done so many times before.

CHAPTER NINE.
SUICIDE

At 1835 hours on 23 March 2000, police officers received a phone call from a friend of Jeremy's and dispatched squad cars and a SWAT team. Upon arrival at his apartment, they made telephone contact with Jeremy and spent a considerable amount of time on the phone attempting to dissuade him from killing himself. At 2115 hours, a supervisor took the phone and was just beginning to speak when officers heard a loud report sound from the apartment. The SWAT team shot tear gas into the apartment and forced entry through the apartment door.

The building was situated on a hill on the West side of Hillcrest Avenue south of Braham. The location was a multi-unit apartment with access to each by means of an outside staircase. The entrance opened up into a living room/bedroom combination. There was a single bed placed in the southwest corner of the living room. There were dishes and newspapers everywhere. As if he did not clean up because he simply did not care anymore.

They found the descendant inside with a gunshot wound to the head. Paramedics were summoned to the scene and pronounced Jeremy dead at 2350 hours. One officer made numerous calls to names and numbers found in his address book in an attempt to trace the family of the decedent.

One friend the police contacted said Jeremy had been threatening suicide for years and that he'd always said that he was going to shoot himself with his shotgun. He said Jeremy had been worried about a pending court date for a DUI arrest in Ventura County. He'd told the friend that his parents were dead — as a result of either a plane crash or auto crash. The story of his parent's death was never consistent.

The police called Jeremy's conservator, Kim Giles— but she was not home at the time. They left a message. When Kim returned from an out-of-town trip, she got the message and rushed over to Jeremy's apartment; but the police would not let her go inside or touch anything.

Kim knew there were family members somewhere, but she never looked for or contacted anyone. Her name was listed as a conservator on all of Jeremy's legal papers as well as on his bank account. She had my brother cremated and his ashes scattered at sea in May of 2000.

***

We learned of my brother's death when Mother died and Aunt Nancy did an online search so that we could notify Paul. Instead, we found his death notice. I sent for his death certificate and told my other siblings that Paul was dead. No one could believe it.

Jeremy

His former roommate made a Memory Book for us — that's all we have left of my brother. Old letters, some photos, a few records ...

Not a day goes by that I don't think about my beloved brother. He was only 34 years old — way too young to die. But he will never be forgotten. May he rest in peace....

CHAPTER TEN.
FILMOGRAPHY

The Cable Guy (1996) (uncredited) — played Serf #4

The Story: It's a time-honored urban ritual: Slip the cable guy fifty bucks and you'll get all the movie channels for free. But when Steven Kovacs moves into a new apartment, his Cable Guy is not like the others. He doesn't want your fifty bucks; all he wants is a friend ... and he won't take no for an answer. Steven is about to learn that there's no such thing as free cable.

Jeremy Applegate plays a medieval serf.

Jeremy is wearing a green medieval-times outfit and is on "Matthew Broderick's team." He dresses Matthew Broderick in his battle gear and is seen dragging him away when he falls. Jeremy is only in the medieval times scenes.

Lies of the Heart: The Story of Laurie Kellogg (1994) (TV) — played Strange Teen

Lies of the Heart: The Story of Laurie Kellogg

Filmed in Los Angeles by MDT Productions and Daniel H. Blatt Productions in association with Warner Brothers Television. Executive producers, Daniel H. Blatt, and Judith Paige Mitchell; producer, Sam Manners; director, Michael Uno; writer, Mitchell.

Cast: Jennie Garth, Gregory Harrison, Steven Keats, Francis Guinan, T.C. Warner, Robin Frates, Alexis Arquette, Sharon Spelman, Jeff Doucette, Virginia Keehne, Gina Phillips, Phil Buckman, William Wellman Jr., Robert Cavanaugh, Robert Factor, Heather Lauren Olsen, Mitchell Binder, Ben Block, Douglas Roberts, William Hubbard Knight, Suzanne Dean, Jeremy Applegate, Sara Moonves, Stephanie Sawyer, Elan Rothschild, Melissa Hunter, Haley Osment, Alexander Lester.

Jeremy

Proving there's life beyond "90210," Jenny Garth tackles the tough role of a young bride who, after suffering years of abuse at the hands of her older husband, Bruce (Gregory Harrison), snaps and encourages her teenage friends to murder him. Based on a true story, "Lies" occasionally suffers from low production qualities, but the horrific tales of abuse and the sordid mess that was her marriage are transmitted with great emotional depth.

The telepic starts with Laurie awaiting trial and looking back at the events, aided by an occasional narration. Each prison scene begins in slo-mo with a blue, grainy screen adding to the character looking back in wonderment at how her life has turned out.

The story, spanning ten years, begins with 16-year-old Laurie meeting Bruce in a bar, and as their relationship develops, so does Bruce's obsession with younger women (it is hinted that he was playing more than hide-and-seek with some of the neighborhood kids that Laurie babysat).

Jeremy

It is well established early on that Laurie is a sympathetic character who is naive about life, is devoted to her husband, and will stop at nothing to please him.

He takes terrifying advantage of this; Bruce seems nice but his abusive interior begins to surface little by little until he becomes a monster: beating her, abusing her mentally, and threatening to kill her and their children. The changes in his psyche are realistically developed over a period of time.

Garth does well with the role, suffering only in the far-from-believable, hasty scenes where she is interviewed by reporters on the way to court. Garth is good at the initial teenage innocence required for the role, but there is very little change in her appearance over a period of ten years. Surely someone in makeup could have helped.

Acting. Jeremy plays one of the strange teens helping Laurie Kellogg with the death of her husband. (A very small part)

"Lies" carries a warning — as it should — that the abuse portrayed is shocking, not always from the visually graphic, but from what is hinted at and

Hard Copy — "Too Young to Love" (1993) TV Episode — played Mark Sotka

Jeremy plays a very abusive boy in this movie. He forces himself on the young woman, he takes control of the situation then everything gets out of control. A very good part for Jeremy.

Davis Rules — "The Moment of Youth" (1992) TV Episode — played Mel

Jeremy plays one of the children, Mel in one episode. (a guest on the show for only one episode)

Dwight Davis, a widower and grammar school principal, has the task of raising his three sons, along with the help of his wacky father Gunny. After the series moved from ABC to CBS, the oldest son and his friend were dropped and Dwight's sister was added. Added as well was Skinner, a son of some of Dwight's college pals who moved in. It was explained Skinner's parents were archaeologists located in Latin America. Also, the oldest son was said to have become a foreign exchange student. Appearing occasionally was Dwight's love interest Erika, but she soon ran off and joined a convent.

5. Heathers (1989) — played Peter Dawson

Jeremy Applegate plays Peter Dawson, a student body president handing out papers on teenage suicide.

Jeremy Applegate's career was cut short when he passed away on March 1, 2000, at the age of 34.

Jeremy

Veronica mingles with Heather I, II, and III to be as popular as them, even though she hates them. She hates them enough to wish they were dead, but she would never want to be their cause of death. When she starts dating Jason Dean, however, she finds herself involved in the murdering of most of her enemies, covered up as suicides.

Three high school girls named Heather run an iron-clad social clique at high school. One of their anointees, Veronica, isn't sure she wants to fit into the clique, particularly when she has to snub some of her old friends at the Heathers' behest. When Veronica meets the new guy at school, she starts ...

Jeremy

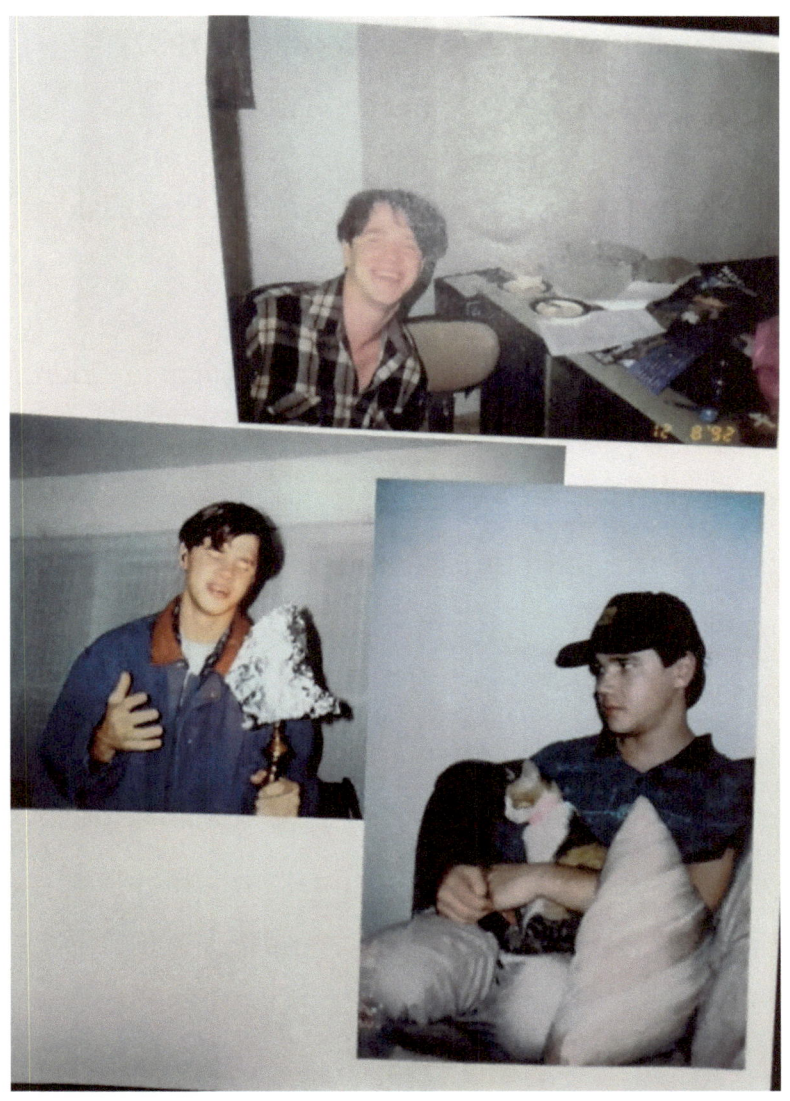

Superior Court — "Yes, Mother" (1987) TV Episode — played Dean Ogden

Jeremy plays Dean Ogden as one of the children (a small part as an extra).

On the heels of the successful "Divorce Court," "Superior Court" was among a wave of reality-based courtroom dramas released in the late 1980s. Both criminal and civil proceedings were presented, with most cases involving shock value rather than routine cases. Examples of cases included a defendant tried for murdering another man, but the defendant claimed he saw the actual perpetrator in a dream; and a man who sued a financial institution after a banker swindled him out of $10 million.

Jeremy

Jeremy

Jeremy

Jeremy

Jeremy

Jeremy

Jeremy

Jeremy

Jeremy

Jeremy

Jeremy

Jeremy

Jeremy

Jeremy

For Paul's Family:

It's always hard losing a loved one, even more so in this way. You will always be in my thoughts and prayers.
God Bless.

— Anonymous

***

For Jeremy:

Heathers is my favorite film, you were such a talented actor. I only wish I could have seen you in more films.

Much love,

— TWY

Paul Donigan

★★★★★

Friend of Jeremy

Reviewed in the United States on August 17, 2020

I worked with him for quite some at Victoria station at universal studios hilltop.. awesome dude.... wish I could contact family so I can them what adventures the 2 of had...

***

It is the hope of all we might have been that fills me with the hope to wish for impossible things.

— P2

I think about you every day Jeremy, and I will forever.

I hear the wind call your name.
It calls me back home again

Jeremy

It sparks up the fire

A flame that still burns ...

I love you and I miss you so much.

— Angie

***

You were a good friend. I thought you were a riot on the set. You taught me how to keep it from getting boring. You are missed. Peace be with you.

— Joe

***

Rest in peace. I'm sorry you took your life. You were a great actor. I love *21 Jump Street* and I heard they're making it into a movie. You are not Forgotten. CYA in Heaven.

— Daredevil

Jeremy

***

Young man, you were such a beloved actor. I'm sorry you thought there was no other way. Rest in Peace. See you in Heaven.

— Mary

***

You were a beautiful person and a bright light. You will live in our hearts always.

— Your Family

***

I didn't know you, but your talent has touched me and so many others. I will never forget you.

— Anonymous

***

Jeremy

What a loss for the world. Thank you for your work. Rest in peace.

— David K.

***

It's such a shame when someone with so much to live for decides they've had enough. My heart breaks. Rest in peace.

— RJ

Jeremy

This is a book of letters that Paul sent me between 1997-1999. There is also a page of the few photos that I have and some blank pages in the back. I thought that as the book is passed around through the family, people can add thoughts and memories and any pictures that they may have regarding Paul to share.

Keep in mind that these letters are just an insight into the history leading to Paul's death. Why He made the choices that he did we will never know. As for advice, I recommend that you find a constructive way to express your thoughts. My advice to Rosemary was art or poetry, and there are other things to do as well. You just have to find one you like.

Jeremy

My deepest regrets to the family,

Jennifer Johann

887 Linden Ave. #A

Carpinteria, CA 93013

805-684-0049

Jeremy

Dear Jennifer,

Hi. I think the trouble with you sleeping all the time could be due to not being on Didrex, Cylert, or Dexedrine. Ask for Dexedrine by name if you can, it's definitely strong enough to keep you awake, and maybe even feel HAPPY. Explain your case history to your Dr (I mean as far as what drugs were tried, etc. But you're on so much stuff now, I wouldn't be surprised that you're tired all the time. Tiredness-Depression.

Thanks a lot for the Roswell book and the Newsweek. I think I'll start the book tonight.

Which pink slip is in the maid's room: BMW, or Cougar? Do you have anything at all that has your license plate and VIN (the numbers you can see looking through the driver's side of the windshield)? Do you have any more paperwork? I would like to get the pink slip because I'm afraid Mrs. Barbey won't release it, and plus I don't know if she has it parked in the garage or not, so I can't just go over there and look for myself unless I have the pink-slip, signed by you. Plus I need the keys. This is just in time...my Hyundai is getting worse every day. I wouldn't be surprised if it gives out next week.

That sounds like some tricycle. Do you look like the chain-smoker at Mrs. Enchinas who takes her rabbit everywhere, or maybe the other one who has all the patches, and the pigtails? That was so funny that time you went out to lunch with Mrs. Barbey and had your hair like that. I guess she must not have liked it, she didn't comment on that.

I just got diagnosed with degenerative disk disorder in my neck. No wonder I'm in so much pain 5 days out of the week. There's nothing they can do for me, except fuse the joints together, but then I would lose mobility and look pretty bad as well.

Try to get the signed pink to me, which will show me the plate and VIN# and will satisfy Mrs. Barbey, because then I'll be armed with the bill of sale. (I'm showing her the $1200.00 one) You're right, it probably is something I can fix.

Sincerely,
Jeremy.

Jeremy

Dear Jennifer,

I just got your letter today. Thank you for the poem.

How's living in Santa Barbara? I hear it's really nice up there. Are you by yourself?

Thank you for allowing me to have the option of buying your Cougar. What are you driving now? You're right about the Hyundai, ever since it got hot here, almost every time I try to start it it won't, and I have to remove the top of the air-cleaner assembly in order for it to get enough air to start. It's definitely messed up, but I still haven't brought it in for the recall notices I got in the mail. Hopefully, the defect relates to my problems, but who knows?

I am enclosing TWO Bills of Sale: One for real, and one to show your grandma because I'm sure she'd never trust my word, and would protest selling it for a dollar because she'd rather have it sit in a white trash yard at your cousin's for years, rusting away. By the way, does it have tail lights now? Fill them both out and return with the pink slip if this is a serious offer.

I need to give you a date of sale and mileage on my BMW. Unless you have already sent in your release of liability for the BMW... I haven't done anything with it. Too poor. I'm renting the same spot at Evelyn's for $25 per month.

I urge you to SUE the Medical Center of North Hollywood for malpractice (you have a perfect case, someone says you OD'd and they wouldn't see you for hours, resulting in you being put on a respirator. I still have that letter I wrote to the medical director if you need it). Jennifer, your silly Dr and his lying bullshit of a reply letter still maintain that you were triaged and treated immediately. You and I know we were sitting for three hours before they'd even take your blood pressure, then the Dr. got angry with me when I told him I found you about 4:45 pm, and by then it was closing in on 9 pm. I explained we had been waiting for hours, but he sides with the asshole COUNT admission clerks. You stand to make a lot of money from either or both cases. Find a lawyer... there are plenty of hungry shark lawyers out there, just find one who will take the cases on "contingency" which means you pay him about a 33% cut of your settlement if you win, and if not, no risk to you, no lawyer fees. I would be fucking furious over this if I were you. Sue the fuck out of them. That's what malpractice is for, and apparently, they neglected to turn you over periodically to maintain blood flow, and because of that, you got paralyzed. (Oh, mention how they sent you out the door and you fell, too.) GO GET 'EM!

I have one scene in the upcoming "Rockford Files" MOW (movie of the week) which should be on TV very soon. It was fun. I got to crash into his beloved ugly Firebird, then I blamed it on him, and then a cop harassed him as well. They let me make up some of my own lines which James Garner liked when he heard them, but the executive producer wouldn't use the line in question because they think it would be bad to portray the 69-year-old actor as being "geriatric" if they let me keep the one about incontinence.

I only got slightly above the minimum SAG wage. That "Long John Silver's" commercial might possibly be airing on the West Coast... they tested it a few times, and I just got another holding fee for its 13-week cycle, so that usually means they intend to use the spot, rather than throwing away a session fee payment to myself.

PEACE

Jeremy

jeremy390@earthlink.net

Aug 20, 1997

Jeremy

Whoa! Hold it! You're going to pay LEH $10,000?! I'm not certain that you are LIABLE OR RESPONSIBLE FOR THESE CHARGES. Before you rush off and write them a check, I would call Medicare/TransAmerica, because usually the way Medicare works is this: Doctors agree to accept a certain flat rate for their services instead of their usual fees because it's a federal law that you can't be held responsible for what Medicare WON'T pay. In fact, if you look at one of your Medicare EOBs (Explanation of Benefits) from LEH, it usually says on the last page of the Medicare statement (not the LEH statement) what was paid to them, then an amount followed by the text "YOU ARE NOT RESPONSIBLE FOR THESE CHARGES." Check it out with them (Medicare/TransAmerica) - their # is also on the EOB. FIRST!!!! That's a fuck of a lot of money, and you really aren't in a position to pay. The money you have may be deemed as your ness. living expenses if you are disabled, so, "Make that call now!" Thank you, sweet spirit.

Jeremy

Another way is to tell them that Mrs. Barbey is responsible and let them chase her down. But I think the first choice is to find out your obligation, if any, to LEH. But ask Medicare, not LEH.

I'm glad to hear that you'll be getting SSI and disability. Isn't it crazy that you can get more from the Govt. than your millionaire family? And it's entirely legal.

Yes, I do enjoy the car. I can tell from the noises it makes sometimes that I'll need new Universal Joints soon. That's much less of a problem than the fucking Hyundai! I welcome the Cougar's problem with open arms. Hey, by the way, the new car has insurance now, but I still need to transfer the policy from the Hyundai to the Cougar. 5.0 means the engine size, measured in liters. I'm sure you've seen a lot of Mustangs with a 5.0 badge on the fender. It's the same engine under the hood. The Cougar has that same engine. I enjoy using this onramp to the 101 at Universal City because it slopes downhill sharply, and I can get it up to 85 with no problem even if I'm low on gas. A few nights ago, however, there was a CHP car hiding, and he saw me and followed me, then pulled me over. (I didn't hear him on my scanner... it's broken.) He did a brief sobriety test and followed me again to the freeway on-ramp, registration. He started to go back to his car, then he got a code 2 high call, and he ran back to me, then asked for his license and registration. The reason you're not getting a ticket is because I have an emergency to attend to. That's the only reason he let me go," and he raced away. I'll be more careful on that onramp now that I know it's a speed trap. I've seen other CHP cars parked there too. My lights were on when I was on the opposite side of the FWY.

Did Sheri offer you an explanation of why you didn't get compensated for your accident?

Yes, I can help you liquidate your funds. Just make sure that everything is liquidated that you can think of so the money you know is the reason they wouldn't help you before. I imagine the rest of your injuries are covered normally under Medi-Cal, but if you find a pharmacy that will do all the paperwork for TAR's (Treatment Authorization Requests), Oh, why don't you use the pharmacy that was helping me with the TAR's? It's called Quality Care RX, and their # is (800) 427-1921. They don't deliver in your area, but I just got off the phone with them and they said they can MAIL your Rx to you in a few days. They were always very helpful and on top of things. I never once ran out of meds. Just have your Dr. call in your Rx's to Quality Care once you are on Medi-Cal, but not before. Your Dr. will then need to write a TAR for each of your uncovered meds, but don't worry, Quality Care will follow up on that for you automatically.

I bought a new motherboard and a Pentium™ 133 MHZ processor for your computer plus 16MB of RAM for it. Everything's installed, I just have a bug or two to work out. Next, I'll get you a 33.6 modem an

Jeremy

SVGA graphics card and SVGA monitor, and perhaps a larger hard disk drive with Windows 95 pre-installed. Then you'll be ready for the internet! The internet is much fun. I got (or rather my friend did, but I'm using it) a military-grade encryption program so that email remains private, you can encode just about any file so no one can read it except you. It's fully automated with the Eudora Light email program... available free on the net, and it's very easy to use. I think you might enjoy Windows 95, it's newer and more advanced, but it's simple to understand. The Windows 95 program itself, however, requires much space, so a bigger hard drive is in order if you want to go that route. I'd suggest at least a 1.2 GIG.

I'm afraid that I sold my last 2 canisters of Tear Gas/Pepper spray, but I could get you some more. That place on Hollywood Blvd for you where we originally got some, plus get you a holster. Your keychain one might work on 1 assailant if your aim is good, but I recommend over-kill, using a police size unit so that you can handle several suspects if needed, with/ no fear of running dry and them knifing you or whatever.

That's very nice of you to offer to fix the BMW, but are you sure you want to shell out too much? I think it will cost as much as $3500 to do the whole bit. Body, engine, paint, interior, replace broken and missing parts, suspension, and stuff. I mean, you already gave me such a great deal on the Cougar.

I'm glad that you are still feeling better. Just remember what it's like to feel that way, and if you start to feel bad again, realize that it is possible to get back to feeling good again because you've already experienced it. Try to remember what combination of things in your life equals feeling ok.

If the neurologist thinks an operation will help, discuss it with him. It might be the way to go, and nerve things can get worse if left untreated. I had thought that you fully recovered. Have you considered what I said about the malpractice suit? I think it would be easy to find a lawyer to take the case because of the blatant neglect the hospital dished out. Not to mention you almost dying in the waiting room.

I'm glad you have a cat to sleep with. Clarice and Febe are doing fine, and are very well-adjusted in this neighborhood. They just need to be careful of coyotes at night, because they come down the hill, looking for prey after dark. I think Febe got chased by one because once I was in the bathroom where the cat came through the tiny window sill, and she came flying through the opening with her fur all puffed out, and she peed on the hammock out of fear. She never makes mistakes like that. I think it was a physical response to being terrified. Other than the fucking coyotes, they have fun bringing in lizard after---

Rx to you in a few days. They were always very helpful and on top of things. I never once ran out of meds. Just have your Dr. call in your Rx's to Quality Care once you are on Medi-Cal, but not before. Your Dr. will then need to write a TAR for each of your uncovered meds, but don't worry, Quality Care will follow up on that for you automatically.

I bought a new motherboard and a Pentium™ 133 MHZ processor for your computer plus 16MB of RAM for it. Everything's installed, I just have a bug or two to work out. Next, I'll get you a 33.6 modem, an SVGA graphics card, an SVGA monitor, and perhaps a larger hard disk drive with Windows 95 pre-installed. Then you'll be ready for the internet! The internet is much fun. I got (or rather my friend did, but I'm using it) a military-grade encryption program so that email remains private, you can encode just about any file so no one can read it except you. It's fully automated with the Eudora Light email program... available free on the net, and it's very easy to use. I think you might enjoy Windows 95, it's newer and more advanced, but it's simple to understand. The Windows 95 program itself, however, requires much space, so a bigger hard drive is in order if you want to go that route. I'd suggest at least a 1.2 GIG.

I'm afraid that I sold my last 2 canisters of Tear Gas/Pepper spray, but I could get you some more. That place on Hollywood Blvd for you where we originally got some, plus get you a holster. Your keychain one might work on 1 assailant if your aim is good, but I recommend over-kill, using a police size unit so that you can handle several suspects if needed, with/ no fear of running dry and them knifing you or whatever.

That's very nice of you offering to fix the BMW, but are you sure that's not going to put you out too much? I think it might be as much as $3500. to do the whole bit. Body, engine, paint, interior, replace broken and missing parts, suspension, and stuff. I mean, you already gave me such a great deal on the Cougar.

I'm glad that you are still feeling better. Just remember what it's like to feel that way, and if you start to feel bad again, realize that it is possible to get back to feeling good again because you've already experienced it. Try to remember what combination of things in your life equals feeling ok.

If the neurologist thinks an operation will help, discuss it with him. It might be the way to go, and nerve things can get worse if left untreated. I had thought that you fully recovered. Have you considered what I said about the malpractice suit? I think it would be easy to find a lawyer to take the case because of the blatant neglect the hospital dished out. Not to mention you almost dying in the waiting room.

I'm glad you have a cat to sleep with. Clarice and Febe are doing fine, and are very well-adjusted in this neighborhood. They just need to be careful of coyotes at night, because they come down the hill, looking for prey after dark. I think Febe got chased by one because once I was in the bathroom where the cat came through the tiny window sill, and she came flying through the opening with her fur all puffed out, and she peed on the hammock out of fear. She never makes mistakes like that. I think it was a physical response to being terrified. Other than the fucking coyotes, they have fun bringing in lizard after lizard. Big ones, baby ones, and every size in between, plus about 5 birds since we've been here. Clarice makes a day out of it. That's her schedule. She'll usually come in with something in her mouth when it gets dark.

That's good that you are going to be working with kids again. I know you enjoy that. If you get overwhelmed, just call in sick. Don't resign like last time. You'll end up feeling better and want to go back, so don't burn your bridges. Today is today. Tomorrow may hold something different.

Oh, the buyer for my Hyundai only offered me $400, so I turned him down. Maybe I'll take it to the dealer for its recall service, then see how it runs, and then sell it for more. Fuck, the stereo system cost about that much! The fuck if I'm letting it go that cheap. He must have thought I was a fucking idiot. I just told him no thank you and walked away.

Do you think I should fix my big nose instead of the BMW? That might be better for my career and self-image, plus I already have to have nose surgery on the inside for a deviated septum next week, but of course, SAG won't allow anything cosmetic, because I'm sure every fucking actor wants a nose job. My *Rockford Files* should be out soon. Watch for it.

No, I still haven't filed the papers to sue that gay mother-fucker director. It just makes me so angry to think about the whole thing that I can't concentrate on writing my complaint.

Jeremy

9-8-97

Dear Jennifer,

So what do I do to do this? Get an estimate on my nose and an engine and suspension/brakes (to start with) on the BMW. As long as you're not going to try to kill me or something like that, I may be able to come set up your computer for you. (When you get that big hard drive?) Just need a faster modem and a bigger hard drive. The other incidentally is nearly done. Just need a faster modem and a bigger hard drive. I bought you an SVGA monitor and graphics card. MUCH improved visibility w/ those components! Your printer keeps spitting out smeared sheets, I replaced the toner cartridge, and this did not help. The printer expert said that it might need a new "photoconductor unit" which is well over $200. I suggest selling it in the recycler and picking up an Epson Stylus Color 600 for the same price, and it will last a lot longer. That's the kind of printer I've been using to write you. It actually prints my headshots sharper than Kinko's. Plus, it's a color printer.

What email address did you use, I didn't receive any mail from you. The address jeremy390@earthlink.net works.

The *Rockford Files* is for Universal. I don't know what network will play it though. I've recovered from my nose surgery and can breathe better now. (I had one side blocked by a deviated septum.)

Do you also want some powerful speakers with your computer too, and maybe get you that big hard drive? The biggest about $250 will buy? Then you can run Windows 95. How about a tape drive for backing up your system for $50? My friend has one that stores up to 4 Gig on one cartridge! Zip drives only hold 100MB each, and that's not much. Plus the cost of the tapes, and it's six times as much as the tape drive I'm recommending. The only difference will be the massively increased storage capacity, and it will be a built-in unit. It's easy to use. Oh, speaking of which, would you want me to take out your Dinosaur 5.25 floppy drive and put the tape drive there? Because otherwise there's no space for it. I've already copied all your 5.25 disks, including software disks to the 1.44 MB floppy. The 5.25 is not very reliable these days.

Is the computer you're using Windows 3.1 or Windows 95? What's your email address? Do you want me to set up an internet account for you on your new Pentium 133 MHZ 16MB RAM computer so that when I bring it to you, it's all set to go? The other type of computer tech you can think that you might want is a scanner. You can find really good ones for about $300 these days! There's no telling what kind of trouble you could get into with scanned prints tied together. (Meaning: you can create and modify shit all you want.) It eliminates your need for a copy machine, and the scanner acts as one anyway with 300 DPI color.

Jeremy

Are you trying to get me to come up there so you can kill me?

Answer that, and let me know about the above-mentioned stuff.

Peace

Jeremy

P.S. Thank you for pot smoking.

Thank you so much for the Cougar 5.0 deal! At last, I can get to my interviews on time, and sweat and grease-free! That engine truly does let me outperform in traffic. When I make some more money, I think I'll put a larger 4 L throttle body on it for about 10-15 more horsepower. Your grandma didn't give me any shit about it and didn't even ask for the pink slip or the bill of sale. Guess what? Since my Hyundai has been parked in the same spot for about 5 days, someone left a note on it wanting to know if I'm interested in selling it. FUCK YEAH! That car's a death mobile, particularly in the section of the city where acceleration and braking are the keys to not getting hit.

The Cougar does have some bumpy vibrational noise at times, but I believe that it's the U-joints (bearings that attach the driveshaft to the tranny and the rear wheels). I'm not complaining though! There was an article in this month's *Road & Track* magazine about replacing Ford U-joints. I noticed that the trim pieces in the back are missing. The parts below the tail light that says "Cougar LS".

Do you know where they are, or give me that dirty bitch lawyer's telephone # who took everything off the car when her dirty body shop didn't put everything back on. Hey, did you ever get the settlement they were dragging out, or did you decide against calling the State Attorney General's office about her? I hope you took Sheri's advice about it. That camel-fuck lawyer is a crook, and she deserves to lose her State Bar license too. Fucking immigrant camel-jockey is trying to take advantage of our fucked-up system in order to pocket more than her clients get! I hate corruption.

Jeremy Applegate

Jeremy Applegate

Thank you sooo much for the Cougar 5.0 deal! At last, I can get to my interviews on time, and sweat and grease-free! That engine truly does let me outperform in traffic. When I make some more money, I think I'll put a larger T-body on it for about 10-15 more horsepower. Your grandma didn't give me any shit about it and didn't even ask for the pink slip or the bill of sale. Guess what? Since my Hyundai has been parked in the same spot for about 5 days, someone left a note on it wanting to know if I'm interested in selling it. FUCK YEAH! That car's a death mobile, particularly in the section of the city where acceleration and braking are the keys to not getting hit. The Cougar does have some bumpy vibrational noise at times, but I believe that's the U-joints (bearings that attach the driveshaft to the frame and the rear wheels). I'm not complaining though! There was an article in this month's Road & Track about how to replace Ford U-joints. I noticed that the trim pieces in the back are missing. The parts below the tail lights that say 'Cougar LS.' Do you know where they are, or give me that dirty bitch lawyer's telephone # so I can have her dirty body shop didn't put everything back on. Hey, did you ever get the settlement check from the auto body shop? You should consider calling the State Attorney General's office about the scam she is prospering in. Those are major felonies, and she deserves to lose her State Bar license too. Fucking immigrant camel-jockey is trying to take advantage of our fucked up system in order to pocket more than her clients get! I hate corruption."

Jeremy

Dear Jennifer,

Sept 25, 1997

What an awesome surprise I had when I checked my savings account balance! I refused to believe it was true until the funds actually became available to me about 4 days ago. I moved my BMW out of Evelyn's garage yesterday, over to the trailer park trash acquaintance I know who is renting a house with two others. They're not going to charge me unless I just let it sit there. I am going to price engines tomorrow. My ear+nose+throat Dr. told me that to narrow my n****r-boy nose, they would have to do some external cutting which may leave small scars. I'll take your advice and see a specialist. Scars and acting don't mix.

It's your computer—tell me what you want, and I'll assemble it for you. The SVGA PCI graphics card and the SVGA monitor make an incredible difference.

Also, now that it's a Pentium 133MHZ, the phone/fax program works perfectly.

Enclosed are the two checks you asked for. I'll also deposit $1,000.00 into your checking tomorrow. It will be in your account by the time you receive this letter. Be careful not to ever have over $2,000.00 in your account, or Medi-Cal will disqualify you.

I feel empowered and protected by the money. Less worries. The only person in the world who knows about it is Dr. Allen. I will never tell anyone else. That will just invite freeloading scumbag friends. So are all your meds being covered? Are you getting the pharmacy to process "TARs" for uncovered meds? At this point, everything should be completely free of charge. You've spent enough money on your meds!

Are you still feeling good? Tell me about a typical day. How's Charlie? Claire rarely comes by now, and the ignores me for the most part. She'll eat and run. I don't know what's worse: her habits, or her better elsewhere in the neighborhood. Maybe she's kicking it at someone else's house. Febe sleeps with me every night, and when I lay down from all the neck and back pain...she's right there to comfort me. She still enjoys smoking pot. There are at least two lizards in my apt right now. I got rid of the roach-infested stove and got my money back, then went out and purchased a new one from Circuit City, and took it off the rent. I'm glad the refund I got for the stove worked. I think all the roaches are gone, but I'm not sure. The health dept has come here twice to inspect, which has kept me from doing any sort of tomato-type projects. I requested a professional exterminator, but my slumlord won't comply. He even lied to the Health Dept and told them I'm allergic to the stuff exterminators use just to get out of paying for them. Can't I ever find a decent landlord? The Health Dept will fine him heavily if he hasn't gotten the exterminators here within a week from now. Roaches are such vile, disgusting creatures.

Jeremy

I got into a big fight with Jimmie over him not paying his fair share of pot. He got really defensive when I brought it to his attention, saying, "OK, I won't smoke any more of yours." Which makes me look like a tightwad asshole, but I can't support his habit. He's clearly UNWILLING to pay his fair share.

Have you been watching "South Park" on Comedy Central? It's a cool animated series about foul-mouthed eight-year-olds. They say things like, "It's not my fault your mom's a dumb stupid bitch." It comes on Wednesdays at 10 pm on Comedy Central. Check it out, it's hilarious.

Go get stoned and go see *Contact* with Jodie Foster ("Yes, Mr. Crawford, sir, very much, very much.")

2810   E.   Del   Mar   Blvd   #7
Pasadena, CA 91107"

Jeremy

Hi,

I noticed that the $1800.00 check I sent you made out to "Forrest" has not cleared. That is not the exact amount, I wrote it for the amount you requested. Didn't you get it? Also in the same envelope, I sent you a long letter and another $50.00 check, what's going on?

Make the evil Peggy's pay. It's a drop in the bucket for them, and they're financially sound. They're your family. If they agreed to pay, then they should. They have millions, literally, and I DON'T! Also, as I've said before, they can't make you pay any amount that Medicare doesn't cover. It's called "accepting assignment" which means they send the claims to Medicare, and Medicare evaluates the charges and pays on their own scale of what they think is fair. IF YOU LOOK AT YOUR MEDICARE "EXPLANATION OF BENEFITS" look down towards the bottom, where it has the unpaid charges, and it should say "You are not responsible for this amount." Just mail them a copy of that.

Your computer now has a 1.2 Gigabyte hard drive, plus the original 420MB drive. I got you some more memories too. I'm going to get you an Epson Stylus Color 600 printer which is PHOTO QUALITY COLOR! I'm going to set you up for a "Learning Windows 95" CD ROM for you, that will teach you how to run Windows 95. It's supposed to be simple and straightforward.

Where or what is the situation of your new home? Is it like a Gabes-type thing, where you get outpatient care?

Do I still get to do my BMW and my nose, or are you just dangling this in front of me to tease me or drive me mad? I'm not complaining, but I'll have to pay substantial taxes on this money. I thought the whole thing was sort of like compensation for my care and the "pain and suffering" sort of deal. You even joked about it. I'm not really sure what's going on. You said and showed that I have good intentions. I'm not an asshole. I wouldn't recommend you paying $8,000.00 to anyone even if it was in your bank account. You are "indigent" (poor) and there's really nothing anyone can do about it. It's a tax write-off for these places. It's all legal to not pay too. Look at your Medicare E.O.B. like I said, and mail them a copy with the text highlighted where it says "You are not responsible for this amount". And if the Peggy's said they would pay, then THEY ARE RESPONSIBLE, NOT YOU! You are not responsible.

Anyway, my fucking neck and back are killing me. I gotta go take some more Vicodin and Norflex. It will probably be pretty soon that I come to visit you.

Jeremy

PEACE

Jeremy

Jeremy Applegate

4845 Whitsett #11

Valley Village, CA 91607

PLEASE FORWARD

Monday, January 05, 1998

Hi dee ho, Jennifer! Gosh, you sure smell nice and flowery!

I got your letter about a week ago, but haven't answered until now because I've been very sick. (Mentally) Dr. Allen has sort of gone into hiding. I haven't had a session with him since Sept. I've only been able to reach him by beeper on a couple of occasions. I might get a new psychiatrist soon, but I'm worried about him being smart and competent.

Yes, computers WILL play music CDs as well as any stereo, with the right speakers. I just got you a Casio MIDI keyboard that has many instruments on it, connects to your computer to record your own music, and even prints out sheet music. Then you can replay it after modifications to the keyboard (which has very loud speakers), or the computer itself. (Getting very loud speakers). I also bought you a 24-bit flatbed scanner, a 56K modem with speakerphone, and fax and voice mail.... (This is a much better program than the problem-plagued one we used to use at Whitsett.)

Sorry it's taking so long to build this damn thing, but better devices keep getting less expensive, so I've already upgraded it several times. I replaced the teeny 420MB Hard Drive and the 1.2 GIG Hard Drive with a nice 3.4Gig Hard Drive. I'm afraid you won't have WordPerfect because that program is for DOS, and your computer now runs Windows 95. But do not worry, I got you Microsoft Word, which is much easier to use. (And has online help) I already got you a CD-ROM that teaches you Windows 95. There is another CD ROM available for the cost of shipping ($5) to teach you MS Word, but I can't get it because it's one of those special offers with one CD per customer.... However, you can call to get the Word CD-ROM yourself by calling (800) 525-7763.

They'll ask you to name a couple of choices... choose MS Word as your free selection, and Windows 95 level two as your evaluation copy. But don't order until you actually have your computer.

What do you want your username to be for your Internet account? Think of several choices, and a password (use upper/lower case, and numbers, at least six digits long.)

I'm going to load your machine up with tons of software. You won't really need anyone to set it up, just plug in the cables, and switch it on. We can email each other regarding help (there are tons of help sites on the Internet).

I can't see an acupuncturist because I fucked up by not showing up for 3 appointments, and he's pissed. I had it done once by someone else, and it worked and felt great, but I have to stick (get it?) with a Dr. from my SAG network.

Yeah, Hyme the pot vacuum has been around, only because I have no friends. I realize the friendship is very transparent, and that he is using me... I've told him to fuck off many times, but he keeps coming back for more. It's the Hyme from Chandler.

Did you see the "South Park" Xmas special? It was hilarious! If your meds are covered, then your Dr is getting you TAR's. Isn't it nice not having to spend $1200? Per month on meds? That shit? I think that Peggy and Linda should pay for everything you want and need. They are fuckers! Use them to your full ability!

Are you going to get therapy and/or surgery to correct your slipped disk? That must hurt like a bitch. My neck and back are all fucked up. I'm managing the pain with a combination of Vicodin, Norflex (a muscle relaxer), a sonic wave device, and an electro-stimulator that works on your energy meridians, a technique similar to acupuncture, only the needles just shock you instead of pricking you. I'm sorry to hear about your leg. Why don't you use North Hollywood Medical Center? You have two very strong cases against them. (Dr. Allen says what they did to you (or didn't do) is malpractice, but don't tell him I told you that info.) Get a lawyer.

I'm glad you're taking classes and stuff. What kind of projects are you working on?

The engine work has just begun on my BMW. I'm pleased that the smog check laws have changed, making my car exempt from testing! I can't find the pink slip anywhere. Do you have it? If not, I may need to apply for a new one. I have enclosed a bill of sale so that I have some proof of ownership. Please sign it and return it with your next letter.

Jeremy

I've been having problems with my cokehead next-door neighbor. I parked in what he claims is "his" parking space, and he left me two nasty notes threatening me. It is not his space; it is regular street parking. The day after the notes, another neighbor called me to tell me that he found my tires from Nevada in the garbage, so I approached the cokehead.

He started screaming and yelling in my face, and became violent, so I took out my tear gas (do you still want some?) as a precaution. He saw this and freaked. I went back inside my Apt. And he tried to force his way in, even leaving a six-inch black shoe mark on my door. The next day I went out to get my mail, and he came outside again and started to provoke me. I again took out my tear gas, and he ran inside and called 911.

Then he came out and said, "Don't go anywhere, they are coming for you!" Then the police showed up (two units) and he started lying and saying that I came to his door and threatened him with it for no reason. He then went on and on about his fucking parking space, and I think the police realized that he was a psycho, because they told me if he gets out of control again to "Give him a good dose of tear gas." They also told me to tell the landlord to have him move and gave me a paper explaining how to get a restraining order.

I called the landlord, but he wouldn't cooperate, so I mailed him a serious letter warning him that he faces a lawsuit if anything happens to me from the neighbor, because of his refusal to remove that fucker from the building. A few days later, the landlord gave me a copy of the 3-day notice he gave the fucker, and wrote me a reply. I have him shaking in his boots. Now the psycho kisses my ass and pretends that nothing ever happened. I guess the threat to throw him out made him change his thinking. He even paid me $10. To give him a ride to get a part for his car! It's really bizarre. But if he fucks with me, I won't be so kind... I'll spray him good, just like the police said to.

Anyway, that's what's up around here. I'll talk to you soon.

Jeremy

Jeremy

Jeremy Applegate

4845 Whitsett #11

Valley Village, CA 91607

Friday, January 16, 1998

Dear Jennifer,

Hi. I just got your letter today. Yes, I was nearly in a hospital or morgue. Holidays suck. I'm trying to get with a new DR. from Las Encinas, but he's been too sick to see me.

I saw myself playing in "Good Will Hunting" too, and recently, I FINALLY got new pictures, and the photographer says I have a "Matt Damon thing going on". (He played Will.)

Why in the fuck do you want to become a county patient? Do you realize what they do to county patients? (I think you remember) It's not worth firing your Dr. who is already getting paid by your family. You can still cut ties with them w/o having them stop paying. Just continue to have ALL your bills sent to those rich, cheap mother-fuckers. I know you hate them, but you need their money....so take it!!!! It doesn't change who you are or anything about you. Please don't go to the county. You need the top doctors around you!

Who pays your bills is irrelevant. So, my strong, thought-out advice to you, is: KEEP YOUR DOCTOR, AND CONTINUE HAVING YOUR RELATIVES PAY. THEY ARE AN INEXHAUSTIBLE SUPPLY OF MONEY THAT YOU VERY MUCH DESERVE HAVING. FORGET ABOUT YOUR FEELINGS ABOUT CURRENCY. WE ALL NEED MONEY, AT LEAST UNTIL THE GRAY'S TAKE US AWAY. DON'T BE DUMB.

You can be independent and still have them pay your way. Don't give that up, because only YOU will suffer, and you've suffered enough. It is their responsibility to take care of you. You don't necessarily have to speak to them or see them. Just send the bills. (Have all the doctors send the bills directly to them so you don't even have to give it another thought.) Please listen to what I'm telling you: I've never steered you wrong in the past, have I?

Also, you should not feel like you don't deserve to get paid for working with kids. You're like anyone else, and it is very odd to have that sort of guilt and worthlessness when countless millions of Americans work, and duly expect to get paid for their time. You are no less deserving. Now that you have heard it said, don't feel bad. If you feel like working, work, enjoy what you're doing, and expect pay just like anyone else. And keep accepting money from your relatives; regardless of what you think. You have to remember that your thinking can become distorted. Listen to me. Go back and re-read what I just wrote to you above. Don't be stupid, I know you are not. Throw away that old tape in your head: Erase it with a large magnet.

Jeremy

Hemp paper kicks ass! Send me a pic of your jumper when you get it. I've never heard of that.

Yeah, I got my neighbor under control, and I also have a new device to defend myself: A Taser!! Yes, the thing the police use....it shoots out two high-velocity electrical darts up to 17 feet, and the darts will penetrate two inches of clothing, including leather jackets! Then it shocks the shit out of you. I have two extra dart cartridges that came with it. When you have expended a cartridge, it operates as a regular stun gun (which I don't have too much faith in) or you can snap on another for your next assailant. I got to get some sort of holster, because I don't want that sucker firing accidently and getting myself! The tear gas is on order still from that place on Hollywood Blvd. He didn't want to sell it to me at first because he said I couldn't carry the police model, so I offered my Tear Gas Certificate, he ordered some, and should notify me soon. I might have to buy six because he was claiming it's not worth it to him to just sell two or three. Oh well, the price we pay to protect ourselves from the scum of the earth.

I'll send you Clarice and Febe pics as soon as they are developed. They haven't changed much in appearance. Febe still looks very young. I guess she takes after me.

Don't worry about the pink slip: I think I can get another one with the bill of sale. Thank you.

Oh, god, the Xmas South Park was so fucking funny!! Hopefully, it will be on again. It was all about jews worshipping shit for Xmas instead of Santa or Christ. There was a live-talking piece of shit throughout the whole episode. He was singing and jumping around in Kyle's bathroom, making brown shit stains wherever he lands.

I got that pic of the old people fucking on the Internet. You can find worse, believe me. Did you like the one lady sticking her hand up another's cunt? It looked like she was in the middle of an excavation of some sort.

Anyway, talk to you soon. I've got to get working on something quick. My disability is going to be reviewed again this year. Plus, I might shoot myself if I slide down too far.

Peace.

HEATHERS 1988

Friday, July 03, 1998

Dear Jennifer,

Things aren't going well at all. The upcoming holiday which will be spent alone pisses me off and makes me sad at the same time. I spent ALL of last years AND this year's holidays by myself. Only New Year's was ok, cause I had a "South Park" marathon to watch, complete with a countdown to 1998. I think humor really helps people. I wish this was more universally recognized as helpful—laughing takes your mind off your problems and can even make you see your own life differently. (Unfortunately, this never lasts long for me.) I'll sit and watch a movie by myself, and laugh out loud very hard at times. (And as you know, I'll laugh at what other people in a movie theater setting would deem inappropriate times.) Fuck 'em. Like I give a fuck.

I was on PCH in my Cougar and a nigger ran in front of the vehicle just ahead of me in the #2 lane. I slammed on the brakes, and was going to veer left, but I was not certain if a car was parallel to me in the #1 lane, and there was no time to look, and the nigger was still in the street, but was moving erratically. I decided to do an evasive maneuver to the right and came to a full stop a Jetta on the shoulder of the road was backing up, reverse lights on, and rapid pace. She slammed into my passenger side front with her driver's side rear. I heard the radiator being torn to pieces in my car by the pushed-in fan. She broke a headlight and headlight assembly, mashed in my bumper, bowed the right front fender—and pushed it into the passenger door, rendering it unopenable by more than about 4 inches—, and as you know from your vast experience in crashing this very same car (hee hee!!), the entire "bib apron" (which is the part that holds the headlights, grill, and side markers) is made of fiberglass and is one piece. So the entire part in front of the hood (minus the undamaged grill and driver's side stuff) must be replaced. Will need bumper or straightening, and without a doubt, a new bumper cover and impact shocks. Plus a fan blade, radiator, and A/C radiator thingee. The Old Gray Cat from Mercury really made the 4 door sedan Jetta into a Rabbbit-like hatchback. At least on the driver's side.

She was partially in the roadway when she backed into me. I pulled my car safely over onto the shoulder, got out, walked to her window, and said "What the hell was that??" The fat black woman behind the wheel said "I was checking a tire." The fat black woman behind the wheel said "I was checking a tire, IF I HAD SEEN IF ANYONE WAS HURT...SHE HAD 2 OR 3 NIG PASSENGERS." The fat Nig said no one was hurt. I said, "Look, you don't drive in reverse on a forward street, highway, freeway, or interstate...even if you're in the breakdown lane. And especially since you were partially in the traffic lane. Let me see your driver's license, proof of insurance, and registration please." The fat nig said, "Oh, don't worry, I have all of that." "Good," I said. "Here's all of my information." (I'm fully insured, liability at double limits, collision, theft, vandalism, and fire. — if you can actually believe that! <THANKS TO JJ!>) She said, "You know you're at fault, right? Whoever rear-ends someone else is automatically at fault, so treat me like a lady!" "Mam, I said, just please give me your information and we'll go our separate ways for now. I'm trying to treat you like a lady, but then you become uncool, then calm, what's up?" "Well, I'm not on any drugs. You can give me any kind of sobriety test you want to." I replied, no, that won't be necessary. I'm not an officer."

I took down her plate number, and asked for her name, because "class" she had left her driver's Lic., insurance, and registration "at home". She said "Tonishia." She said, you know, we don't really need the cops for this, but if you don't treat me right..."

"Hey! Look, you have everything you need from me. Just cooperate. And by the way, I have no problem with the police being summoned. I'm insured. No warrants." I asked for her last name, and she walked away and told one or more of her passengers "that we need to put this in so-in-so's name as the driver." I said, "No, I don't think so. She supplied me with a last name and a number, and said she'd call me later that night. Then she got into her car and attempted to flee the scene. I could have Tazed and/or tear-gas/pepper-sprayed her, but I thought I'd just call 911 down the street, if the Cougar could make it without overheating and blowing the engine. I at least had the plate #. Then just as she started to leave, I got into the Cougar and started it, again hearing the fan make the radiator into julliane French fried potatoes. Then, for the first time in my life, I was very happy to see pretty red and blue lights in my mirror. I shut off the protesting engine, and got out. 3 more police units shortly arrived separated us, and got our stories. Since there were no apparent injuries (but ever since I have had more pain than usual in my neck and upper back.) the Oxnard Police took no report. They cited the fat black Nig Bitch for driving without a licence, and **let her go!** LAPD would have cracked her skull open and arrested her ass, and impound the car. They did make one of her licenced passengers drive, though.

Jeremy

The Oxnard Police called for AAA tow (also AAA is my insurance co.) While they were waiting with me until the tow came, we talked shop a bit. They were interested in my arsenal of self-defense weapons. Especially the Tazer. They didn't touch or unholster any of my weapons, but they wanted to look in my "fanny-pack" <Fuck, I hate that gay name! Do you know what else to call those?> for a gun. They were cool about it though. We talked about how LAPD had killed a Nigger by Tazering him while he was standing in the water of a swimming pool. Remember that?

They also liked my CHP Proximity Detector. They'd never heard of such a thing. -This is an actual car/base station scanner that has special circuitry built in to check 154.9050 every 2 seconds (The same theory of my handheld scanner we used to listen to for static on that frequency to accomplish the same "sniffing out the CHIPPIE.") and if there's any activity, it sounds a LOUD alert and turns on a BRIGHT red light to indicate the presence of the CHP. It works in all 48 states. And it's legal. It also comes preprogrammed with every police, fire, ambulance, Highway Patrol, aircraft, CB, Dept of Transportation (DOT), and even the local weather, wherever you may be. You know that book of frequencies for police I have? Well, I randomly chose about 200 frequencies and tried programming the scanner for them...THEY WERE ALL IN THERE ALREADY! It's saved me countless times. Except, ironically, when I actually went to the Post Office to p/u the BearTracker scanner, I was racing along a street near the freeway. BearTracker scanner, I was racing along a street near the freeway at about 80 in a 35. In the Cougar. The BMW wasn't running yet. The street I raced along on is always wide open with traffic signals usually in your favor. The problem was, that there was a CHP on the freeway, and he said I was passing him by. He got off and pulled me over. He gave me a speech, and then gave me a ticket for 50mph in a 35mph zone which was nice of him, I guess. He asked for the registration, and I couldn't find it, but I knew it was in the trunk. He came back to the window, and said "Sign in the red box". I said, well, what about this registration thing? I got it in the trunk. "Sign in the red box." He insisted. The fucking fine for that, even though my registration was current, and I brought a copy of it to show the court clerk, was $165.00 - and that's just for the no proof of registration. I argued the point with the clerk, but since the CHP pig decided to checkmark the box on the citation "non-correctable" when it IS a correctible offense, that part of the citation should be treated properly as "Correctable". No sale. $165.00, please. As you know, I had a perfect driving record until the ticket...which I decided would be hard to fight, particularly because he knew I was really going 80MPH. So I went to traffic school. $70 to the court, plus whatever the traffic school charges. But: I found out you can do your traffic school on your home or office or friend's computer by signing up, ($35. - not too bad) they give you their WWW (World Wide Web) address, a personal passcode, and you can do it at your own pace, (so long as you complete the course and pass the tests by the court-ordered deadline.) save your work, and it takes less time to complete, depending on your knowledge, and you don't have to be bored for two 6-hour in-class study with a bitter, angry disabled or retired cop as your instructor. Technology rocks. I have a Mutual Fund that invests in emerging growth new technology, and medical and technical advances. I found out too late that I have no say so in what corporations they invest my money in stocks. But Glendale Federal talked me into it, saying that I shouldn't be happy with the low interest rate the money was earning in my savings. So far, my fund has only lost me money.

Either Chin (the owner of this building) or a "neighbor" complained to DOT that a BMW was abandoned. I found a warning card on my BMW about moving your car at least a mile every 72 hours or they can take it. I drive the mother-fucker at least every other day! On the warning card, they wrote down the last 3 digits of my odometer, (which is broken <or was at the time>) I can understand it looks like an abandoned vehicle... (It got bodywork, and a new driver's door, and some parts are primer gray, some still black, and the door is gold, so I can see how they would think it's a piece of shit, but I just put a fucking $3000.00 engine under the hood!) Anyway, the same meter maid came back a week later, and impounded my BMW for being "parked or stored on a public street for 72 hours or more." It was parked there for exactly a fucking half an hour!! I got it out, ($160. later) and promptly got a used speedometer and cable from that cool BMW junkyard you know about. He wrote me up an invoice, reflecting the frozen mileage, and then I had a friend type a Deposition (statement of facts) stating that we had driven the car the very day they impounded it and that I complained about the parking warning, and that he noticed neither the speedometer or odometer was working. Plus I had my insurance that I bought for it in Jan, again showing the same mileage.

Any idiot would come to the conclusion that the evidence strongly suggests that the car HAD NOT been parked from May 21 through May 29th, unmoved. But I received a letter after presenting my evidence at the impound hearing, and they said "IMPOUND WAS FOUND TO BE VALID AND JUSTIFIED."! Then I presented the same evidence to the Parking Violations Bureau, and they said the same thing!! Fuck, that fucking pisses me off when someone decides I'm guilty when I am clearly and totally innocent!!!!!!

Finally, as you know, the owner/landlord must change the door locks with each new tenant. When I first moved in, that's the first thing I asked. He said, "No. The guy that used to live here gave me back the keys." I didn't want to push the issue because it was so fucking hard and so outrageously expensive to move here, I was just relieved to have a roof over my head (That turns out, leaks badly). So, I took it upon myself to purchase and install new locks. About 2 weeks ago, I lost my keys to my APT. But I wasn't locked out, so I thought they must be lost in my mess of a room, but after many frustrating hours of digging, only to found a dead mouse and a dead lizard. Nice. So I re-keyed one lock to save Chin money and bought a better quality lock for the bottom. I took it off my rent. Chin accepted the check, then later called me and told me he couldn't and wouldn't pay for locks because I lost the keys. True, but he never replaced the locks when I first moved in, as required by law. I tried to explain this to him, and all I heard was "You lost the keys." So finally, I was so pissed off I called him a slant-eyed fucking gook. (He's originally from China) He didn't return any of my calls since then. A few days later, the rent check I gave him was slipped under my door. No note, no explanation. I called him and left 5-6 messages offering him a choice: accept my check minus the lock money, or accept my rent in full, and I will take you to small claims court for the locks. No returned calls. Nothing. Then on May 11, he gave me a 3 Day Notice To Pay or Quit. It was unsigned. (Also slipped under my door) I again called and offered him a choice, and warned him that he was treading on thin ice. No response. On May 26, at fucking 4:15 AM I got served with eviction papers. It said if I didn't respond in 5 days, the Sheriff would remove me forcibly. This affected me badly, made me suicidal, depressed, unable to sleep, vomiting, 102-degree temp, high blood pressure, 120 beats a minute (I was trying to get my allergy shots; they checked me out...that's how I know the figures mentioned.) They refused to give me my allergy shots because they were afraid something adverse would happen. The nurse was so personally worried that she begged me to drive home (but first tried to get me to take a cab) and to "please please call me when you get home so

I know you're safe, and drink lots of juice, and see the Dr. first thing!"

It's nice to have someone actually care about what happens to me. Even if they are just medical people trying to limit their liability, I did sense some sincerity in her.

It was hell trying to get legal advice. Many of the programs to assist low-income citizens/and help fight evictions were shut down. I finally found one place, and she said she couldn't get me in until after the 5 days expired, which meant I'd have to do everything myself. Then I mentioned putting a gun in my mouth (a truism) so she said to come on Friday. As you might imagine, there were many niggers and Mexicans. It was horrible. No A/C...I got a heat stroke and felt like I might have a seizure, so I went to their bathroom to puke...just in time. Some of the barf didn't quite make it into the bowl.

Jeremy

They interviewed me and gave me a list of things to get, such as, certified copies of all complaints, warnings, and citations at my address from the Building & Safety and County Health Dept. Also pictures of the condition of the building, and my unit. I went back on Monday...the day I had to respond to the suit, and they said they would represent me in court. Good deal.

By the way, the morning I read the eviction papers, I went to the bank and got a cashier's check for the full rent, and mailed it by certified mail, return receipt. I got the return receipt on Saturday. Then on Monday, I received the cashier's check back in my mailbox. (He used a stamp this time...Chin is well known here for stuffing notes and envelopes COMPLETELY inside everyone's mailbox. He gave me a copy of the 3-Day Notice that way, so I called the Postmaster. He said not only is this improper service of legal papers, but **IT IS A FELONY FOR ANYONE OTHER THAN THE RESIDENT OR THE POSTMAN**

TO PUT OR TAKE ANYTHING OUT OF SOMEONE'S MAILBOX! I fucking hope they prosecute this mother-fucker. They even gave me a case number, so maybe they will actually charge him with a felony. It would be icing on the cake for me if he is an illegal alien as well. Deportation time! Time to go over to China and get run over by a tank!

Well, Jennifer, sorry to complain about all of this, but this may be the end of me. I'll fight to the end, but if I lose, I will kill myself. I've lived in at least 24 different places since first arriving in LA in 1984. I don't have the energy, nor the inclination to find another place...especially when the court rules against me, because I will only have 5 DAYS to move!! Plus, Clarice is still missing. Febe and I are waiting for her to walk through that window at any moment. I even have a motion sensor in the bathroom where the cats come in so that I will know immediately if she shows up. So far it's Febe and this fucked-up male cat who still has his balls. I think some cold heartless mother-fucker abandoned him. He cries out loudly to announce that he is coming into Febe's space. I feed him because it doesn't seem like anyone else does. I don't want him inside because his scent may be driving Clarice away...this cat showed up 2 weeks before Clarice ran away. Clarice hates him. Also, the mother-fuckin' cat will purr, and then walk over to my bed, jump on top, look cute, then suddenly he fucking takes a god-damn piss on my bed. He has pissed on other things too. I'm tempted to take some scissors and castrate him myself. The vet wants $80, then I'd have to let him stay inside for his post-op healing with all his fucking fleas, and his scent may make Clarice think that she's been replaced or shut out. I had posters up of Clarice around the neighborhood, but some asshole keeps taking them down. No one has called, even though I lied and said she needs meds, and that there is a reward. I suspect someone adopted her and wants to keep her. She had a tag with my name, address, and phone, as well as the vet's. The other possibility is that she was killed by a car, or eaten by a coyote. If I have to move, it means I'll never see Clarice again for certain.

So, for now, I have to wait for the trial to see if I get to continue to live here.

The cool neighbor who used to work at an auto body shop for 8 years who was going to do all the bodywork and primer on my BMW is back East, indefinitely. I did get the bodywork done for $400. (plus $100.00 for the door, and $85 for the rear panel.) but it still needs to be primed and painted. I've got new high-performance BMW 2002 parts in unopened boxes crowding my APT. I have Bilstein Sport shocks, Suspension Techniques Sway Bars, and stiffer, lower springs.

Remember how badly deteriorated all the door, trunk, window seals and weatherstripping were/are? I got a weatherstripping package for the car, with all the rubber on the whole BMW 2002 (windshield and glass seals, door gaskets, trunk gaskets, etc.) Except for the gas, clutch, and accelerator pedal rubber, and of course, no tires! The whole pack was insanely priced at $580.00. (Remember, we are only including the rubber weatherstripping stuff!) which I think is utterly crazy—my springs and shocks cost less than that. ...But my BMW expert at the junkyard said that's a deal, particularly since all but two pieces are "OEM" (Which means "Original Equipment Manufacturer" which means that BMW made the parts. NEW as if the 2002 is still in production.) I'm told I could have saved some money by getting copies of the factory pieces, but they also tell me anything but OEM is taking a big risk. I'm going to try to do the suspension and brakes this w/e, but I need an important few items like wheel bearings and seals, and new flexible brake lines.

Back to the brakes: The calipers I have on the front now are only single piston (or if you prefer, one plunger.) units, with one brake line per front wheel.

The calipers of the BMW 633csi are FOUR PISTON per caliper. And there are TWO brake lines supplying them with fluid, rather than one, which is a nice safety feature in case a hose blows. Plus, the 4 calipers working together, squeezing that shiny round part of the brakes, (the rotor) which is a vented rotor off a 320i, gives a huge advantage, not only will you not need to press on the brakes as hard as the stock 2002 brakes, but you have all that extra reserved braking power for control and safety. 4 piston calipers on both front wheels exert massive pressure, halting the same vehicle in a much shorter distance than ever before. I might go one step further and get stainless steel brake lines that will never swell, leak, or burst. Unless of course "Dog Shit Boy" comes by with a metal cutter and damages it. I'm concerned that Jimmie might have told Tyler where I live, because I haven't called or seen or heard from Jimmie in at least a month or more. I'm holding out. I don't need to call him, lonely or not. He's not a positive influence. He puts me down when I quote lines from movies, or if I talk about my Dr. or my meds, he is just also rude, and says things like, "You really think you're funny?" "Why is it that you always have problems?"

Anyway, I have much to worry about. I hate feeling ok and then suddenly my mood changes and I hate myself, and everyone who has ever hurt me. Then I want to take it all out on myself. I have been sleeping the whole daylight time of the days away about 3-5 times per week. I had two auditions for a commercial and for a short little director's reel. I got up late, and rather than call my agent and admit I fucked up by already having to be at the auditions 1-2 hours earlier, I just went back to sleep. It sucks. At least Febe loves me, and I love her. She's a very sweet kitty. I feel bad that her mama has run away. I'm going to put up new posters as soon as I finish programming this computer (this computer is yours.) You now have a "SuperDisk 120MB Internal"

Removable media disk drive. Treat it as your "A:" drive. That's what it replaces. It's really cool because it is "backwards compatible" with the everyday normal 1.44MB 3.5-inch floppy disk you have come to love and know. I trashed your 5.25 drive. As you may or may not know, ordinary 3.5 disks only hold 1.44MB. This new LS-120 SuperDisk holds 120MB! That's 20% more storage than the over-rated "Zip" drives. And, the special 120MB 3.5 LS-120 disks are extremely inexpensive compared to its more popular, competitor's cost for Zip Disks. (These two media are not compatible with each other.) Also, the LS-120 "A:" drive is not controlled by the very slow floppy interface. It's connected to an IDE controller...the same interface that runs your hard disk drive and your CD ROM.

Well, I'm off to smoke a bowl, and maybe clean my APT. Write soon.

If I come see you and bring your computer and give you a quick run-down on it, and how to get help...on the computer itself. There are walk-throughs, tours, tips, etc. You can always insert the Windows 95 CD ROM, and when the menu comes up, choose the "tour" or "explore this disk." Will you promise me that you won't be clingy and weird, and let me have a little "buffer zone" around me? And please don't ask me to make promises to come back on such and such date, and that you won't ask for my telephone # and all that? I know you miss me, I'm not trying to be cruel, I am only following Dr. Allen's strict guidelines when I many times discussed 7% of my investment, to be exact. And that's just in 3.5 months! If I want to pull out now to avoid losing more money, I have to pay my broker 5% .....something they didn't share with me upfront. So I have no choice but to leave the money alone and hope my Mutual Fund doesn't continue to lose money. I feel stupid about this. There are many legitimate online traders that only charge you a fee per transaction, usually $9.95 for up to 100 shares, depending on the stock-trading service. I wish I would have gone that route. All but about $2000.00 is tied up right now, and I'd be embarrassed to tell you the pitiful balance of my funds. Where the fuck did it go?

Yeah, I did smoke a lot of pot, but still! (I would have grown some by now, but I have had Building and Safety and Health Inspectors here on and off all the time because my slumlord won't fix stuff.) Incredibly, the owner asked me if I ever tried MJ before for my neck and back pain, and I said Yes. He said, "My wife has arthritis and she smokes it too." "Ok!" I said, "Would you keep it to yourself if you came by one day and I had just ONE pot plant growing for my own use?" He said "I don't care. I don't need to tell the police anything." I thanked him, but the situation has drastically changed since then. Building & Safety and the County Health Dept. has fined him, and forced him to repair things. He is dragging his feet, and not complying with Building & Safety's or the Health Dept's demands. I did fuck him over well by reporting the illegal garage conversion to an "APT" and after the inspector left, the guy that lived in the conversion had to move in 3 days! I feel sorry for him, but on the other hand, I did do something very gracious for him. I have a Landlord/Tenant Handbook from the city, and it stipulates that if someone has to move because of unsafe, or illegal whatever, the owner has to pay the person $2000.00 to $5000.00 (5000.00 if you're disabled, or have a minor dependent on your taxes, $2,000 to all other folks!) I hope he comes back to get his mail. It's still in there, as far as I know.

Now for my next disaster (OH, I never finished...they declared the Cougar a total loss, and they will probably give me shit for money.) That pisses me off, because I've seen what you have done to it more than once, and this isn't as serious!

Jeremy

Jeremy

Jackie, Dennis, Paul, Dad and Brian

STATE OF CALIFORNIA
CERTIFICATION OF VITAL RECORD

COUNTY OF LOS ANGELES • REGISTRAR-RECORDER/COUNTY CLERK

CERTIFICATE OF DEATH
STATE OF CALIFORNIA

3 2000 19017081

DECEDENT PERSONAL DATA	1. NAME OF DECEDENT—FIRST (GIVEN) JEREMY	2. MIDDLE E.	3. LAST (FAMILY) APPLEGATE	
	4. DATE OF BIRTH MM/DD/CCYY 05/10/1968	5. AGE YRS. 31	7. DATE OF DEATH MM/DD/CCYY 03/23/2000	8. HOUR 2350
	8. STATE OF BIRTH CA	10. SOCIAL SECURITY NO. 556-83-4372	11. MILITARY SERVICE No	12. MARITAL STATUS NEVER MARRIED	13. EDUCATION—YEARS COMPLETED 12
	14. RACE CAUC.	15. HISPANIC No		RPSG TALENT SERVICES
	17. OCCUPATION ACTOR	18. KIND OF BUSINESS ENTERTAINMENT		19. YEARS IN OCCUPATION 10

USUAL RESIDENCE	20. RESIDENCE—(STREET AND NUMBER OR LOCATION) 3160 HOLLYCREST DR APT#8			
	21. CITY LOS ANGELES	22. COUNTY LOS ANGELES	23. ZIP CODE 90068	24. YRS IN COUNTY 16	25. STATE CA

INFORMANT	26. NAME, RELATIONSHIP KIMBERLY GILE-FRIEND	27. MAILING ADDRESS 535 VENICE WAY VENICE, CA 90291

SPOUSE AND PARENT INFORMATION	31. NAME OF SURVIVING SPOUSE—FIRST -	32. MIDDLE -	33. LAST (MAIDEN NAME) -
	31. NAME OF FATHER—FIRST UNK	32. MIDDLE -	33. LAST APPLEGATE	34. BIRTH STATE UNK
	35. NAME OF MOTHER—FIRST UNK	36. MIDDLE -	37. LAST THOMAS	38. BIRTH STATE UNK

DISPOSITION(S)	39. DATE MM/DD/CCYY 05/26/2000	40. PLACE OF FINAL DISPOSITION RESIDENCE OF KIMBERLY GILE 535 VENICE WAY VENICE CA 90291

FUNERAL DIRECTOR AND LOCAL REGISTRAR	41. TYPE OF DISPOSITION(S) CR/RES	42. SIGNATURE OF EMBALMER NOT EMBALMED	43. LICENSE NO.
	44. NAME OF FUNERAL DIRECTOR AFTERCARE CA CREM & BU SOCIETY FD-1166	46. LICENSE NO.	47. DATE MM/DD/CCYY 05/23/2000

PLACE OF DEATH	101. PLACE OF DEATH Residence	102. IF HOSPITAL, SPECIFY ONE	103. FACILITY OTHER THAN HOSPITAL	104. COUNTY Los Angeles
	105. STREET ADDRESS—(STREET AND NUMBER OR LOCATION) 3160 Hollycrest Dr. #8			106. CITY Los Angeles

CAUSE OF DEATH	107. DEATH WAS CAUSED BY: (ENTER ONLY ONE CAUSE PER LINE FOR A, B, C, AND D)			
	IMMEDIATE CAUSE (A) Shotgun Wound Of Head			108. DEATH REPORTED TO CORONER Yes
	DUE TO (B)		Immed.	108. CORONER'S CASE NO. 2000-02245
	DUE TO (C)			109. BIOPSY PERFORMED No
	DUE TO (D)			110. AUTOPSY PERFORMED No
	112. OTHER SIGNIFICANT CONDITIONS CONTRIBUTING TO DEATH BUT NOT RELATED TO CAUSE GIVEN IN 107 None			111. USED IN DETERMINING CAUSE No
	113. WAS OPERATION PERFORMED FOR ANY CONDITION IN ITEM 107 OR 112? IF YES, LIST TYPE OF OPERATION AND DATE No			

PHYSICIAN'S CERTIFICATION	114. I CERTIFY THAT TO THE BEST OF MY KNOWLEDGE DEATH OCCURRED AT THE HOUR, DATE AND PLACE STATED FROM THE CAUSES STATED. DECEDENT ATTENDED SINCE / DECEDENT LAST SEEN ALIVE MM/DD/CCYY MM/DD/CCYY	115. SIGNATURE AND TITLE OF CERTIFIER	116. LICENSE NO.	117. DATE MM/DD/CCYY
		119. TYPE ATTENDING PHYSICIAN'S NAME, MAILING ADDRESS, ZIP		

CORONER'S USE ONLY	I CERTIFY THAT IN MY OPINION DEATH OCCURRED AT THE HOUR, DATE AND PLACE STATED FROM THE CAUSES STATED.	120. INJURY AT WORK No	121. INJURY DATE MM/DD/CCYY 03/23/2000	122. HOUR 2115	123. PLACE OF INJURY Residence
	118. MANNER OF DEATH Suicide	124. DESCRIBE HOW INJURY OCCURRED (EVENTS WHICH RESULTED IN INJURY) Self Inflicted			
	125. LOCATION (STREET AND NUMBER OR LOCATION AND CITY, ZIP) 3160 Hollycrest Dr. #8 , Los Angeles 91025				
	126. SIGNATURE OF CORONER OR DEPUTY CORONER	127. DATE MM/DD/CCYY 05/22/2000	128. TYPED NAME, TITLE OF CORONER OR DEPUTY CORONER Rachel Zaragoza Deputy Coroner		

STATE REGISTRAR				FAX AUTH. NO. 195/7519	CENSUS TRACT

156

Jeremy

STATE OF CALIFORNIA
CERTIFICATION OF VITAL RECORD

COUNTY OF LOS ANGELES · REGISTRAR-RECORDER/COUNTY CLERK

AFFIDAVIT TO AMEND A RECORD   3200019017081
DEATHS AFTER 1-1994
NO ERASURES, WHITEOUTS, OR ALTERATIONS

3 052000 092031

STATE FILE NUMBER

STATE/LOCAL REGISTRAR USE ONLY				

PART I   INFORMATION TO LOCATE RECORD—TYPE OR PRINT IN BLACK INK ONLY

NAME AS IT APPEARS ON RECORD	1. NAME—FIRST (GIVEN)	2. MIDDLE	3. LAST (FAMILY)
	JEREMY		APPLEGATE

ADDITIONAL INFORMATION TO LOCATE RECORD	4. SEX	5. DATE OF EVENT—MM/DD/CCYY	6. CITY OF OCCURRENCE	7. COUNTY OF OCCURRENCE
	M	03/23/2000	LOS ANGELES	LOS ANGELES

8. FATHER'S NAME AS STATED ON ORIGINAL   9. MOTHER'S NAME AS STATED ON ORIGINAL
UNK. · APPLEGATE   UNK. · THOMAS

PART II   STATEMENT OF CORRECTIONS—NO ERASURES, WHITEOUTS, OR ALTERATIONS

	10. CERTIFICATE ITEM NUMBER	11. INFORMATION AS IT APPEARS ON ORIGINAL RECORD	12. INFORMATION AS IT SHOULD APPEAR
LIST ONE ITEM PER LINE	40	RESIDENCE OF KIMBERLY GYLE 535 VENICE WAY VENICE CA 90291	AT SEA OFF THE COAST OF ORANGE COUNTY
	41	CR/RES	CR/SEA
		2 OF 2	

REASON FOR CORRECTION   13. TO CHANGE FINAL DISPOSITION

AFFIDAVITS AND SIGNATURES   We, the undersigned, hereby certify under penalty of perjury that we have personal knowledge of the above facts and that the information given above is true and correct.

TWO PERSONS MUST SIGN THIS FORM	14. SIGNATURE OF FIRST PERSON	15. TITLE/RELATIONSHIP TO PERSON IN PART I	16. DATE SIGNED—MM/DD/CCYY
	►	FUNERAL DIRECTOR	06/16/2000
	17. AGE ADULT	18. ADDRESS (STREET, CITY, STATE, ZIP) 10559 VICTORY BL. NORTH HOLLYWOOD, CA 91606	

USE BLACK INK ONLY	19. SIGNATURE OF SECOND PERSON	20. TITLE/RELATIONSHIP TO PERSON IN PART I	21. DATE SIGNED—MM/DD/CCYY
	►	SECRETARY	06/16/2000
	22. AGE ADULT	23. ADDRESS (STREET, CITY, STATE, ZIP) 10559 VICTORY BL. NORTH HOLLYWOOD, CA 91606	

STATE/LOCAL REGISTRAR USE ONLY	24. SIGNATURE OF STATE OR LOCAL REGISTRAR	25. DATE ACCEPTED FOR REGISTRATION—MM/DD CCYY
	► Office of State Registrar of Vital Statistics	08/16/2000

TE OF CALIFORNIA, DEPARTMENT OF HEALTH SERVICES, OFFICE OF STATE REGISTRAR   VS 24.0.1 (Rev. 1/96)

This is to certify that this document is a true copy of the official record filed with the Registrar-Recorder/County Clerk.   SEP 1 4 2004

Conny B. McCormack
CONNY B. McCORMACK
Registrar-Recorder/County Clerk

19-0899607

This copy not valid unless prepared on engraved border displaying Seal and Signature of the
Registrar-Recorder County Clerk.

ANY ALTERATION OR ERASURE VOIDS THIS CERTIFICATE

157

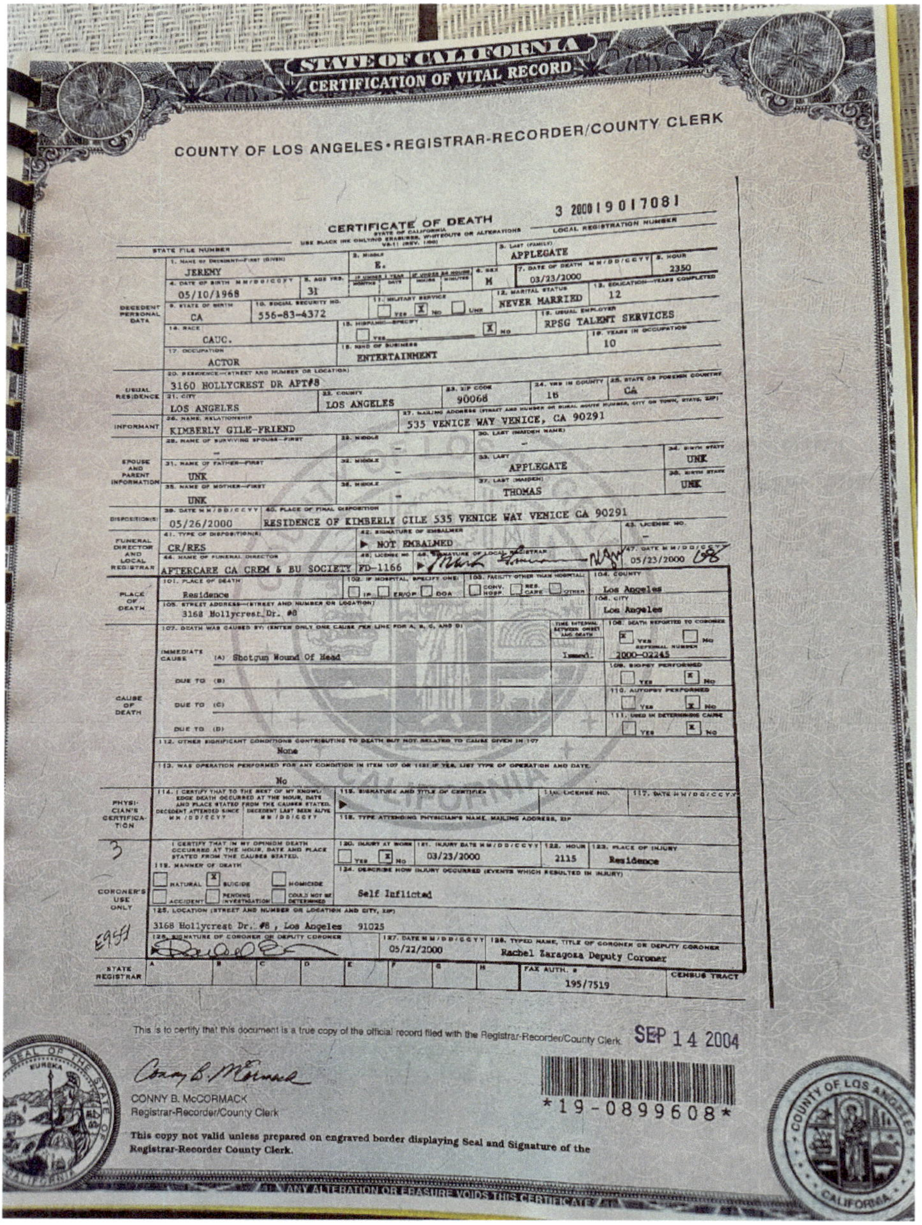

Jeremy

159

Jeremy

DEPARTMENT OF CORONER

MEDICAL REPORT

COUNTY OF LOS ANGELES

SUICIDE

15

AUTOPSY CLASS: ☐ A ☐ B ☐ C ☒ Examination Only D

Date _07/24/2000_ Time _1200_ Dr. _GOLDEN_ (print)

FINAL ON _12/25/2000_ By _GOLDEN_ (print)

APPROXI-MATE INTERVAL BETWEEN ONSET AND DEATH _immediate_

DEATH WAS CAUSED BY: (Enter only one cause per line for A, B, C, and D)

IMMEDIATE CAUSE
(A) _SHOTGUN WOUND OF HEAD_

DUE TO, OR AS A CONSEQUENCE OF
(B)
DUE TO, OR AS A CONSEQUENCE OF

(C)
DUE TO, OR AS A CONSEQUENCE OF

(D)
Other conditions contributing but not related to the immediate cause of death:

☐ NATURAL ☒ SUICIDE ☐ HOMICIDE

☐ ACCIDENT ☐ COULD NOT BE DETERMINED

If other than natural causes
HOW DID INJURY OCCUR? _Self-Inflicted_

WAS OPERATION PERFORMED FOR ANY CONDITION STATED ABOVE: ☐ YES ☒ NO

TYPE SURGERY _____ DATE _____

☐ ORGAN PROCUREMENT ☒ TECHNICIAN _R. LICK_

☐ WITNESSES TO AUTOPSY ☐ EVIDENCE RECOVERED AT AUTOPSY
Item Description:

PRIOR EXAMINATION REVIEW BY DME
☒ BODY TAG _2_ ☐ CLOTHING
☒ X-RAY (No. _2_) ☒ FLUORO
☐ SPECIAL ☐ MED. RECORDS
PROCESSING TAG
☒ AT SCENE PHOTOS (No. _4_)

TYPING BLOOD TAKEN BY _____
SOURCE _____

TOXICOLOGY

☐ NO BLOOD
☐ Embalmed
☐ >24 hr in hospital
☐ Decomposed
☐ Other _____ Reason _____

SPECIMENS
Collected by _GOLDEN_
☐ HEART BLOOD ☒ STOMACH CONT
☒ FEMORAL BLOOD ☐ BRAIN
☐ _____ BLOOD ☐ SPLEEN
☐ _____ BLOOD ☐ KIDNEY
☐ BILE ☒ VITREOUS
☐ LIVER
☐ URINE ☐ _____

STORAGE JARS
☐ Regular (No. _____) ☐ Oversize (No. _____)

Histopath Cut: ☐ Autopsy ☐ Lab

☐ NO TOXICOLOGY REQUESTED

TOXICOLOGICAL ANALYSES ORDERED
SCREEN: ☒ C ☐ H ☐ T ☐ S
☐ ALCOHOL ONLY
☐ CARBON MONOXIDE
☐ NEOGEN SCREEN
☐ OTHER (specify drug and tissue)

REQUESTED MATERIAL ON PENDING CASES
☐ Police Report
☐ Tox ☐ Med History
☐ Microbiology ☐ Histo
☐ Radiology Cons. ☐ Investigations
☐ Consult on ☐ Eye Path. Cons
☐ Brain Submitted
☐ Neuro Consult ☐ DME to Cut
☐ Criminalistics
☐ GSR

Resident _____

DME _____

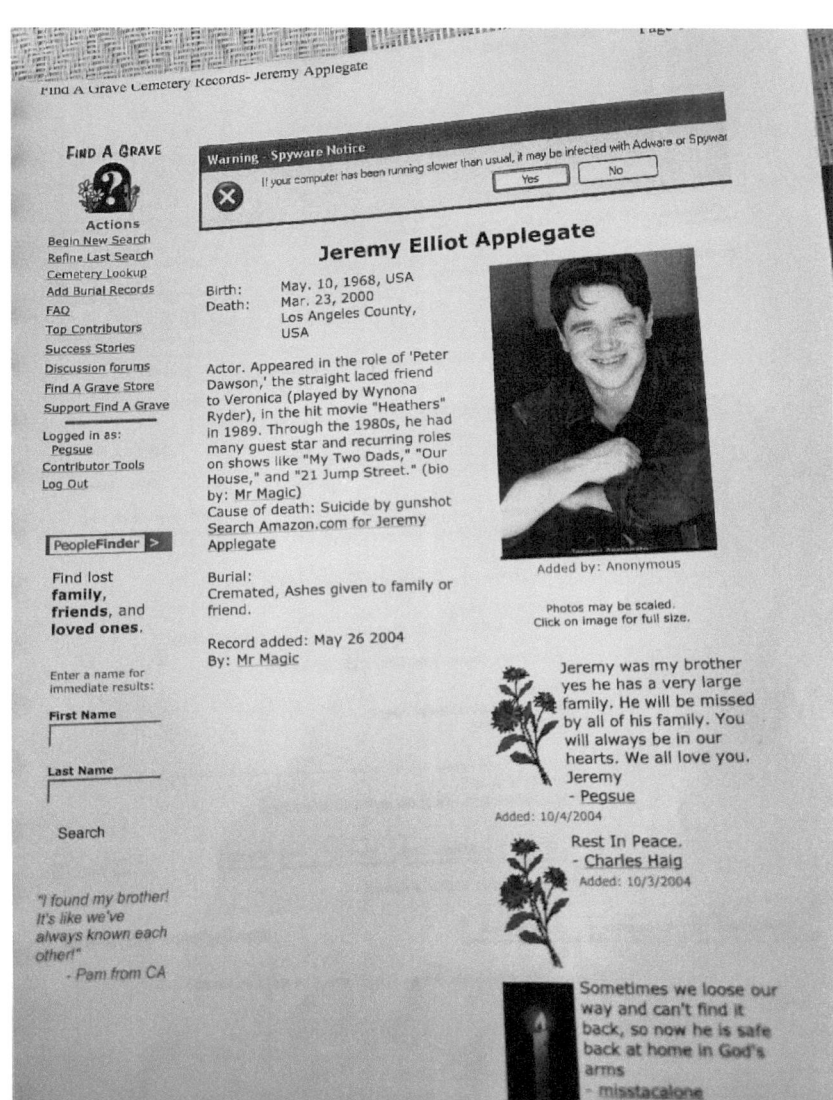

FIND A GRAVE

Actions
Begin New Search
Refine Last Search
Cemetery Lookup
Add Burial Records
FAQ
Top Contributors
Success Stories
Discussion forums
Find A Grave Store
Support Find A Grave

Logged in as:
Pegsue
Contributor Tools
Log Out

PeopleFinder >

Find lost
family,
friends, and
loved ones.

Enter a name for
immediate results:

First Name

Last Name

Search

"I found my brother!
It's like we've
always known each
other!"
- Pam from CA

Warning - Spyware Notice
If your computer has been running slower than usual, it may be infected with Adware or Spyware
Yes   No

Jeremy Elliot Applegate

Birth: May. 10, 1968, USA
Death: Mar. 23, 2000
Los Angeles County,
USA

Actor. Appeared in the role of 'Peter
Dawson,' the straight laced friend
to Veronica (played by Wynona
Ryder), in the hit movie "Heathers"
in 1989. Through the 1980s, he had
many guest star and recurring roles
on shows like "My Two Dads," "Our
House," and "21 Jump Street." (bio
by: Mr Magic)
Cause of death: Suicide by gunshot
Search Amazon.com for Jeremy
Applegate

Burial:
Cremated, Ashes given to family or
friend.

Record added: May 26 2004
By: Mr Magic

Added by: Anonymous

Photos may be scaled.
Click on image for full size.

Jeremy was my brother
yes he has a very large
family. He will be missed
by all of his family. You
will always be in our
hearts. We all love you,
Jeremy
- Pegsue
Added: 10/4/2004

Rest In Peace.
- Charles Haig
Added: 10/3/2004

Sometimes we loose our
way and can't find it
back, so now he is safe
back at home in God's
arms
- misstacalone

Jeremy

JEREMY APPLEGATE:

10/4/2004

Just talked with Kim Gills, about Paul she said that she has known him since he was 14 years old. He was in and out of mental hospitals for years. He had a mental imbalance; he changed his name in 1981 in Bend Oregon from **Paul Andrew Boyce** to **Jeremy Paul Boyce**. He asked Kim to cremate him if he died. Kim was out of town when the police called. The police found Kim's phone number on a piece of paper in his apartment. Kim returned the phone call to the police. She tried to enter the apartment but the police said she couldn't take anything. He had a long history of repressed memories that he couldn't talk about. All his cars were sold and personal belongings were thrown out. He really didn't have any friends; she kept really to himself. He had very highs and lows. His ashes were scattered at sea in La County, California. Kim was a very nice lady and it really helped me with some closure on some things that happened to Paul. I know it was very terrible and seems very unbelievable that he committed suicide. He was a very troubled person. We may never find out the true story or why he never kept in contact with his family. But at least we are having some kind of closure on Paul. May his soul rest in peace. We all will miss you, Paul.

YOUR SISTER

Peggy Gomez

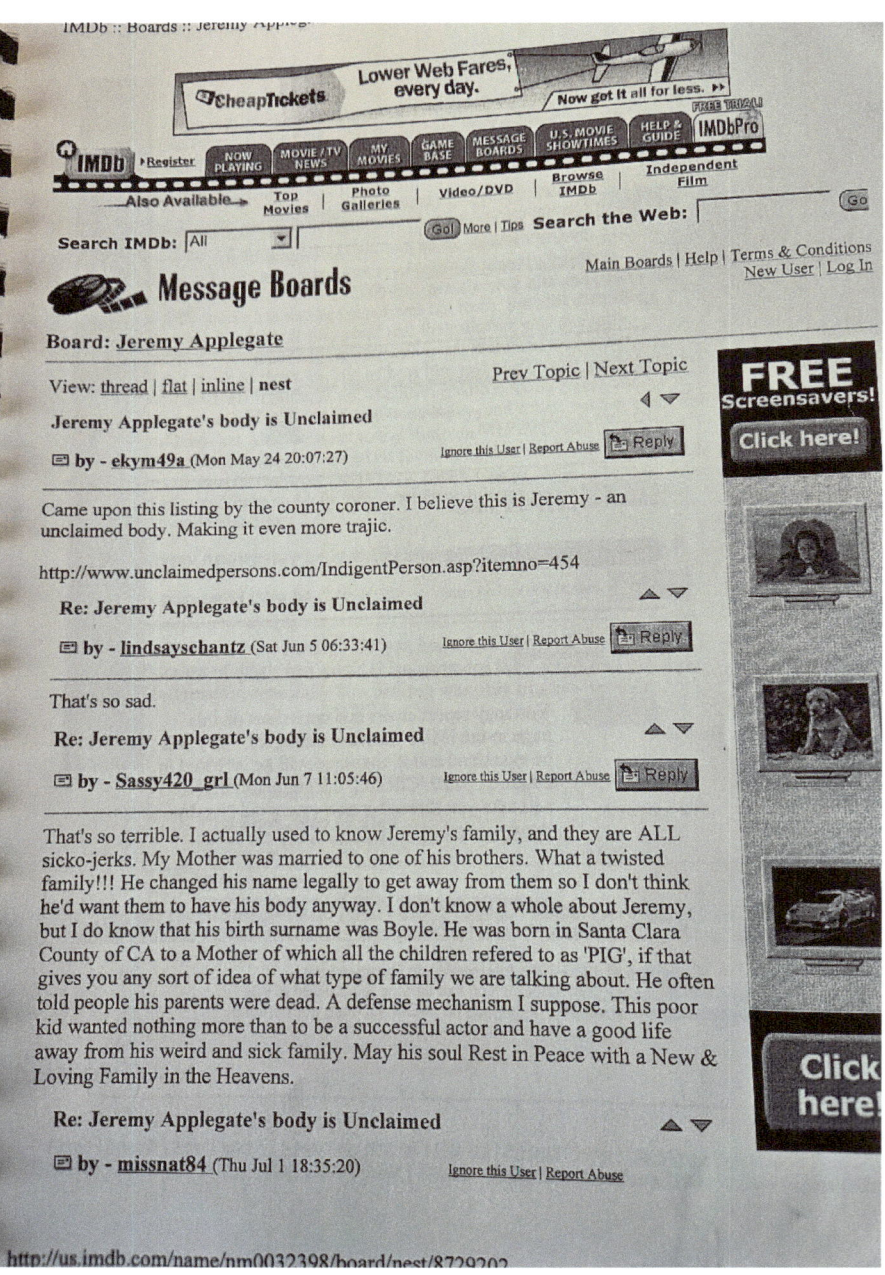

IMDb ►Register | NOW PLAYING | MOVIE/TV NEWS | MY MOVIES | GAME BASE | MESSAGE BOARDS | U.S. MOVIE SHOWTIMES | HELP & GUIDE

Also Available → | Top Movies | Photo Galleries | Video/DVD | Browse IMDb | Independent Film

Search IMDb: All ▾ | Go! More | Tips Search the Web: | Go

Main Boards | Help | Terms & Conditions
New User | Log In

Message Boards

Board: Jeremy Applegate

View: thread | flat | inline | **nest**

Prev Topic | Next Topic ◀ ▽

Jeremy Applegate's body is Unclaimed

✉ by - **ekym49a** (Mon May 24 20:07:27)   Ignore this User | Report Abuse | Reply

Came upon this listing by the county coroner. I believe this is Jeremy - an unclaimed body. Making it even more trajic.

http://www.unclaimedpersons.com/IndigentPerson.asp?itemno=454

Re: Jeremy Applegate's body is Unclaimed ▲ ▽

✉ by - **lindsayschantz** (Sat Jun 5 06:33:41)   Ignore this User | Report Abuse | Reply

That's so sad.

Re: Jeremy Applegate's body is Unclaimed ▲ ▽

✉ by - **Sassy420_grl** (Mon Jun 7 11:05:46)   Ignore this User | Report Abuse | Reply

That's so terrible. I actually used to know Jeremy's family, and they are ALL sicko-jerks. My Mother was married to one of his brothers. What a twisted family!!! He changed his name legally to get away from them so I don't think he'd want them to have his body anyway. I don't know a whole about Jeremy, but I do know that his birth surname was Boyle. He was born in Santa Clara County of CA to a Mother of which all the children refered to as 'PIG', if that gives you any sort of idea of what type of family we are talking about. He often told people his parents were dead. A defense mechanism I suppose. This poor kid wanted nothing more than to be a successful actor and have a good life away from his weird and sick family. May his soul Rest in Peace with a New & Loving Family in the Heavens.

Re: Jeremy Applegate's body is Unclaimed ▲ ▽

✉ by - **missnat84** (Thu Jul 1 18:35:20)   Ignore this User | Report Abuse

http://us.imdb.com/name/nm0032398/board/nest/8729202

Jeremy

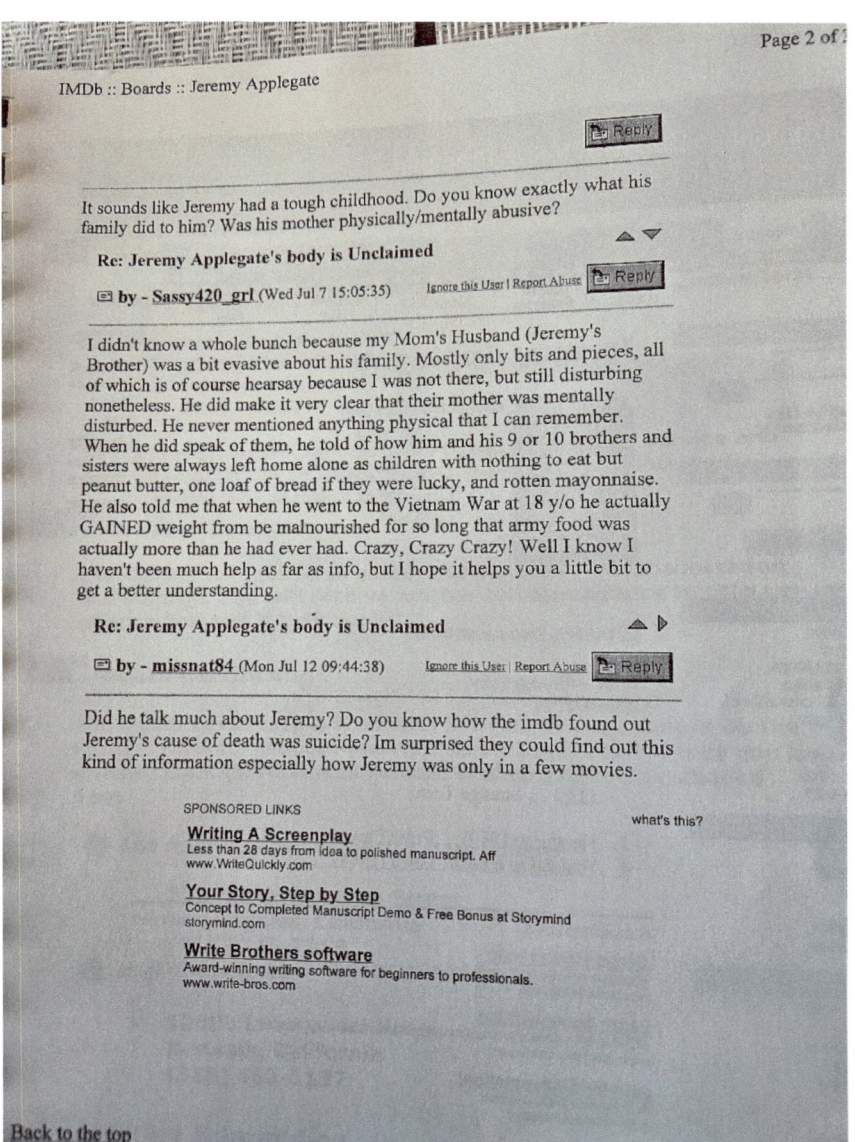

IMDb :: Boards :: Jeremy Applegate

Reply

It sounds like Jeremy had a tough childhood. Do you know exactly what his family did to him? Was his mother physically/mentally abusive?

Re: Jeremy Applegate's body is Unclaimed

by - **Sassy420_grl** (Wed Jul 7 15:05:35)   Ignore this User | Report Abuse   Reply

I didn't know a whole bunch because my Mom's Husband (Jeremy's Brother) was a bit evasive about his family. Mostly only bits and pieces, all of which is of course hearsay because I was not there, but still disturbing nonetheless. He did make it very clear that their mother was mentally disturbed. He never mentioned anything physical that I can remember. When he did speak of them, he told of how him and his 9 or 10 brothers and sisters were always left home alone as children with nothing to eat but peanut butter, one loaf of bread if they were lucky, and rotten mayonnaise. He also told me that when he went to the Vietnam War at 18 y/o he actually GAINED weight from be malnourished for so long that army food was actually more than he had ever had. Crazy, Crazy Crazy! Well I know I haven't been much help as far as info, but I hope it helps you a little bit to get a better understanding.

Re: Jeremy Applegate's body is Unclaimed

by - **missnat84** (Mon Jul 12 09:44:38)   Ignore this User | Report Abuse   Reply

Did he talk much about Jeremy? Do you know how the imdb found out Jeremy's cause of death was suicide? Im surprised they could find out this kind of information especially how Jeremy was only in a few movies.

Back to the top

165

www.ingramcontent.com/pod-product-compliance
Lightning Source LLC
Chambersburg PA
CBHW040850120626
46547CB00006B/560